Benjamin Kennicott

The ten annual Accounts of the Collation of Hebrew MSS of the Old Testament

Begun in 1760, and Compleated in 1769

Benjamin Kennicott

The ten annual Accounts of the Collation of Hebrew MSS of the Old Testament
Begun in 1760, and Compleated in 1769

ISBN/EAN: 9783337067427

Printed in Europe, USA, Canada, Australia, Japan

Cover: Foto ©Lupo / pixelio.de

More available books at **www.hansebooks.com**

O F

THE COLLATION OF HEBREW MSS

OF THE

OLD TESTAMENT;

Begun in 1760, and compleated in 1769:

By

BENJ. KENNICOTT, D.D. F.R.S.

Member of

The Royal Society of Sciences, at GOETTINGEN;

The Theodore - Palatine Academy, at MANHEIM;

The Royal Academy of Infcriptions &c. at PARIS;

Keeper of The RADCLIFFE Library,

And Fellow of EXETER College, in

O X F O R D.

Sold by Mr *Fletcher* & *Prince*, in Oxford; Mr *Woodyer*, in Cambridge; Mr *Rivington*, *Payne*, *Dodfley*, and *Fletcher*, in London. M DCC LXX.

2

TO

ALL THE

MUNIFICENT PATRONS

OF

THIS WORK

THE PRESENT COLLECTION

OF THE

SEVERAL ANNUAL ACCOUNTS

OF ITS PROGRESS

IS

MOST GRATEFULLY

INSCRIBED.

THE

INTRODUCTION.

THE Collation of the Hebrew MSS of the Old Teſtament being now finiſhed, I think it my duty to expreſs myſelf moſt truly thankful — firſt, to DIVINE PROVIDENCE; for that ſhare of Health, which I have enjoyed (tho' of late frequently interrupted) in perhaps too cloſe an attention, during Ten Years, to a Work of ſuch peculiar labour and fatigue — and ſecondly, to all thoſe Illuſtrious and Learned PERSONS; who, with a public ſpirit which has no parallel in the ſupport of any literary under-taking, and with a piety which exceeds all praiſe, have thus liberally ſupported a Work, not expe-dient only, but neceſſary, for the Honour of REVELATION.

As I entered upon this important Work, re-ſolved to proſecute it with all the expedition, and all the care, in my power ; the proper advances made in it, from year to year, gave me ſincere pleaſure. At the end of the firſt, and every ſuc-ceeding year ; I thought it neceſſary, for my own credit in the diſcharge of my Truſt, as well as the ſatisfaction of my Subſcribers, to preſent Them with a printed Account, both of the Progreſs made,

made, and the Encouragement granted. And one of the moſt agreeable rewards, which I could poſſibly receive during this hard labour, has been the Approbation, with which theſe annual Accounts have been honoured by my Patrons : eſpecially, as their Approbation has been followed by the Applauſe of the Learned in almoſt every part of Europe.

Being now to conclude the ſeveral ſhort hiſtories of this Collation, with an Account of the laſt year ; I have been perſuaded to republiſh, and prefix, the Accounts of the nine years preceding. It is no wonder, that ſome of thoſe Gentlemen, whoſe zeal for my Work led them to ſubſcribe to it, ſhould think the annual Accounts worthy of preſervation : and yet it would have been ſtrange, if ſeveral of thoſe little pamphlets had not been loſt, thro' different accidents. This has been the caſe ; and I have frequently been applied to, with ſome earneſtneſs, for other copies of theſe Accounts, in order to make Sets compleat : which requeſts I have ſometimes been unable to comply with, as all the copies for a few of the years had been before given away. A deſire therefore to oblige all my Subſcribers, to the utmoſt of my ability, is the apology I have to offer for this Republication ; and I ſhall beg leave to introduce it with a few hiſtorical particulars.

Soon

Soon after my entrance in this Univerſity, when I learnt the Hebrew language from the celebrated Dr HUNT, Regius Profeſſor of the Oriental languages; I then was, and continued for ſome years, ſtrongly prejudiced in favour of the *Integrity* of our Hebrew Text: taking it for granted (as men of learning far ſuperior to mine did, almoſt univerſally, thro' Europe) that, if the printed copies of the Hebrew Bible at all differed from the Originals of Moſes and the Prophets, the variations were very few and quite inconſiderable.

But, in defiance of theſe prejudices, I became convinced in the year 1748, that our Hebrew Text had ſuffered from tranſcribers, at leaſt as much as the copies of other antient writings; and that there are now ſuch corruptions in this ſacred volume, as affect the Senſe greatly in many inſtances. The particular Chapter, which extorted from me this conviction, and which was benevolently recommended to my peruſal (for this very purpoſe) by the Reverend Dr LOWTH, now Lord Biſhop of Oxford, is the 23d Chapter of the 2d Book of *Samuel.*

Having been thus convinced of my own miſtake, in a matter of ſo much moment; I thought it my duty to endeavour to convince others. And accordingly, in 1753, I publiſhed a Diſſertation on the latter part of that Chapter, beginning at the 8th verſe; which verſe ſeems to contain more and greater miſtakes than are perhaps to be found elſewhere,

where, among the fame number of words. To the remarks on this chapter I added (by way of Second Part) an account of SEVENTY Hebrew MSS, which I had then difcovered; and I fpecified feveral inftances of their Various Readings, which indeed I found to be both numerous and important.

This difcovery of fo many *written* copies, hitherto entirely unknown or unattended to, differing fo effentially in many inftances from the *printed* copies of the Old Teftament, ftruck every reader with furprife. Whilft the more learned, and the more candid, of thefe readers were led to exprefs their warm wifhes — that no farther time might be loft, than had been loft already, in delaying the perfect examination of MSS, which were found to be capable of fuch public advantage.

In the year 1758, when the Delegates of the Prefs at Oxford, with very laudable intentions, requefted the feveral Proffeffors to recommend to them fuch Works, as they thought would be moft acceptable to the Public, and which it would be moft honourable for Them to encourage the publication of; our Hebrew Proffeffor recommended various particulars, the firft of which was *A Collation of all thofe Hebrew MSS of the Old Teftament, which were preferved in the Bodleian Library.*

The Right Reverend Dr SECKER, then Lord Bifhop of Oxford, and late Arch-Bifhop of Canterbury

bury (by whofe death this Work has been deprived of its firft Patron, and has loft His Grace's
farther Recommendation, as well as the ufefulnefs
of His Advice) was fo thoroughly convinced of
the great importance of fuch a Collation, that He
preffed me ftrongly to undertake it. And indeed
He was the Perfon, not only who firft endeavoured
to perfuade me (in 1757) but alfo who chiefly
prevailed with me (in 1760) to give up my life to
this laborious Undertaking. In the year 1758,
His Lordfhip honoured me with a Letter, from
which the following is an extract.

Sir,   Deanery of St Paul's; Mar. 10, 1758.

I have long wifhed, that the Hebrew MSS of
the Old Teftament at Oxford were collated — if
you are willing to undertake it, I think you the
fitteft ; and am glad the Delegates have pitched on
you. I prefume you would have been glad, if they
would have made propofals to you, rather than
have defired you to make propofals to them : but
what Advice would be proper in either cafe, I am
unable to fay — If an annual Salary be propofed ;
it will probably be expected, that the number of
Years for compleating the Work fhall be fixed —
I hope, whatever Doubts or Difficulties may arife,
the Defign will not be foon abandoned, from de-
fpair of getting thro' them—This is all that occurs
at prefent to

Your loving brother and fervant,

Tho. Oxford.

B

Soon after the receipt of this letter, His Lord-ship was advanced to the See of Canterbury; and His Grace then wrote to me, as follows.

Sir,

I am very willing to take the part, which I thought was proper for the late Arch-Bifhop, of confulting with the other Bifhops, concerning fome proper method of encouraging the Undertaking propofed to you — What their opinion may be, I cannot fay beforehand — when I am able, I will give you farther information. In the mean while preparing for the prefs the Work, which you mention, I think will be a very proper employment. I wifh you good Succefs in it, and am &c.

The Work, mentioned by His Grace, was *A Second Differtation on the printed Hebrew Text*, which I publifhed in the beginning of the year 1760; having then feen 110 MSS of the whole, or parts, of the Hebrew Bible. And in confe-quence of the additional difcoveries therein made, I was ftill more ftrenuoufly exhorted by feveral Great Perfons, and in particular by the Arch-Bifhop of Canterbury, to enter upon the Collation of thefe MSS. I confented; and publifhed Pro-pofals. And, after HIS GRACE had begun an Annual Subfcription, for the fupport of this Work; I applied to the *Delegates* at OXFORD, who readily patronized it likewife: as did alfo feveral learned Individuals, and fome Colleges, in this Univerfity.

Thefe

These examples were soon followed by the Universities of CAMBRIDGE and DUBLIN; and by many other learned Men, with some other respectable Societies. And that the Public may not be at a loss to know, *Who were the Persons*, to whom they are indebted for setting on foot this Undertaking; it will be consulting the satisfaction of the Public, and my own gratitude, to give here an exact List of these Subscribers, during the first year 1760.

The University of OXFORD . .	£ 40	0	0
The University of CAMBRIDGE	30	0	0
The University of DUBLIN . .	30	0	0
His Grace, Dr Secker, A-Bp Canterbury	10	10	0
His Grace, Dr Gilbert, A-Bp York .	10	10	0
His Grace, Dr Cox, A-Bp of Cashel .	10	10	0
Rt Honourable, The Earl Granville .	5	5	0
Rt Honourable, The Earl of Macclesfield	5	5	0
Rt Honourable, The Earl of Bath . .	5	5	0
Rt Rev. Dr Sherlock, Ld Bp of London	10	10	0
Hon. & Rt R. Dr Trevor, Ld Bp Durham	10	10	0
Rt Rev. Dr Hoadly, Ld Bp Winchester	10	10	0
Rt Rev. Dr Mawson, Ld Bp Ely . .	5	5	0
Rt Rev. Dr Willes, Ld Bp Bath and Wells	5	5	0
Rt Rev. Dr Thomas, Ld Bp Lincoln .	5	5	0
Rt Rev. Dr Osbaldiston, Ld Bp Carlisle	5	5	0
Rt Rev. Dr Thomas, Ld Bp Salisbury .	5	5	0
Hon. & Rt R. Dr Drummond, L.B. St Asaph	5	5	0

Rt Rev. Dr Pearce, Ld Bp Rochefter	5	5	0
Rt Rev. Dr Hayter, Ld Bp Norwich	6	6	0
Hon. & Rt R. Dr Cornwallis, L.B. Litchfield	5	5	0
Rt Rev. Dr Keene, Ld Bp Chefter	5	5	0
Rt Rev. Dr Johnfon, Ld Bp Worcefter	5	5	0
Rt Rev. Dr Ellis, Ld Bp St David's	5	5	0
Rt Rev. Dr Hume, Ld Bp Oxford	5	5	0
Rt Rev. Dr Egerton, Ld Bp Bangor	5	5	0
Rt Rev. Dr Terrick, Ld Bp Peterborough	5	5	0
Rt Rev. Dr Young, Ld Bp Briftol	5	5	0
Rt Rev. Dr Chenevix, Ld Bp Waterford	3	3	0
Rt Honourable, Ld Tyrawly	2	2	0
Lord Chief Baron Parker	5	5	0
Rev. Dr Gregory, Dean Chrift-Church	5	5	0
Rev. Sir Philip Hoby, Dean Ardfert	3	3	0
Rev. Dr Squire, Dean Briftol	2	2	0
Rev. Dr Webber, Dean Hereford	2	2	0
Rev. the Dean and Chapter of Briftol	5	5	0
Rev. the Dean and Chapter of Durham	10	10	0
Rev. the Dean and Chapter of Exeter	5	5	0
Rev. the Dean and Chapter of Gloucefter	5	5	0
Rev. the Dean and Chapter of Wells	5	5	0
Rev. the Dean and Chapter of Worcefter	5	5	0
All Souls College	5	5	0
Eton College	5	5	0
Exeter College	5	5	0
Jefus College, in Oxford	5	5	0
Merton College	5	5	0

Rev. Dr Afhton 3 3 0
Rev. Mr Atherton 2 2 0
Rev. Dr Atwell 4 4 0
Dr Avery 2 2 0
Hon. and Rev. Mr Aylmer 2 2 0

Rev. Dr Barnard 4 4 0
Hon. and Rev. Mr Barrington . . . 2 2 0
Thomas Bafket, Efq; 6 6 0
Rev. Dr Bentham 1 1 0
Rev. Dr Blackett 2 2 0
William Blackftone, Efq; 1 1 0
Rev. Dr Butler 2 2 0

Rev. Dr Chandler 1 1 0
Mr John Channing 2 2 0
Rev. Dr Chapman 1 1 0
Dr Collet 1 1 0
Rev. Mr Cracherode 2 2 0

Peter Delmè, Efq; 5 5 0
Rev. Dr Dickens 2 2 0

Rev. Dr Eyre 1 1 0

Rev. Dr Fanfhaw 2 2 0
Richard Fuller, Efq; 5 5 0

Rev. Dr Golding 4 4 0
Charles Gray, Efq; 2 2 0
Rev. Mr Greet 1 1 0

Dr Heberden 5 5 0
Frafer Honeywood, Efq; 5 5 0
John Howard, Efq; 2 2 0

Rev. Dr Jennings	2	2	0
Rev. Dr Jubb	2	2	0
James Lambe, Efq;	5	5	0
Matthew Lee, Efq;	2	2	0
Rev. Dr Legh (Halifax)	3	3	0
Thomas Llewelin, Efq;	2	2	0
John Loveday, Efq;	1	1	0
Rev. Dr Lowth	4	4	0
Rev. Dr Markham	4	4	0
Rev. Dr Milles	2	2	0
Rev. Mr Moore	1	1	0
Rev. Dr Mofs	2	2	0
Jofeph Mufgrave, Efq;	2	2	0
Rev. Dr Plumptre	5	5	0
Rev. Mr Prieft	1	1	0
Rev. Dr Pyle	1	1	0
Rev. Dr Randolph	1	1	0
Rev. Dr Salter	3	3	0
Rev. Mr Sanford	2	2	0
Rev. Dr Saunders	2	2	0
Hon. and Rev. Dr Talbot	5	5	0
Rev. Dr Taylor (Chancellor)	2	2	0
John Thornton, Efq;	5	5	0
Hon. Thomas Townfhend, Efq;	5	5	0
Rev. Mr Twynihoe	1	1	0
Richard Warner, Efq;	1	1	0
Philip Carteret Webb, Efq;	2	2	0
Samuel Wegg, Efq;	2	2	0

Thus honourably countenanced and fupported, I entered upon my Work : chearfully devoting the active part of my life to this important Undertaking; determining to exert the utmoft of my endeavours to ferve the Public ; and not at all doubting of the generofity of the Public, for the reward of my Labours. But here ; that no more may be inferred from this Undertaking, than was really intended ; and that the author may not be fuppofed to have promifed what was out of his power to perform, (*i. e.* to collate all the MSS of the Hebrew Bible in Europe) it may be neceffary to ftate, that the Undertaking was precifely this ——*to collate all the MSS of the Hebrew Bible in Great Britain and Ireland* (all fuch as fhould be difcovered, and the ufe of which could be obtained, if defired;) *and, whilft this Work was carrying on* (which it was fuppofed might require at leaft *Ten Years*) that *Collations of as many of the beft Foreign MSS fhould be procured, as Time and Expence would allow.*

Such was my Undertaking. And now, as to the manner in which it has been conducted ; how far properly, or the contrary — this has been already (as far as Nine Years) fubmitted to T h e S u b s c r i b e r s : and the Whole is here prefented to T h e m, and fubmitted alfo to all others, who fhall perufe *The Ten Annual Accounts,* which now follow in their order, and exactly as they were before printed.

ACCOUNT I.

At the End of the Year 1760.

PROPOSALS having been publifhed laft *January*, relative to a Collation of the MSS of the facred Hebrew Text; and fuch an Undertaking having been honoured with great Encouragement from the Univerfities of OXFORD, CAMBRIDGE, and DUBLIN; from the ARCH-BISHOPS, and moft of the BISHOPS in *England*; from fome DEANS and CHAPTERS, and fome COLLEGES; and alfo from feveral PERSONS, eminently diftinguifhed by their Rank and Station, as well as by their Zeal for Religion and Learning: *Mr Kennicott*, who has been employed to undertake a Work of fo public a nature, thinks himfelf obliged (at the clofe of the firft year) to offer fome particulars to the confideration of the Public. And he apprehends, that the Method moft conducive to the Satisfaction of the *prefent*, and the Encouragement of *future* Subfcribers to this extenfive and laborious Undertaking, will be — to ftate the Expediency of fuch a Collation, as in the former Propofals; and then, to mention fuch Circumftances as have occurred, worthy of notice, during the prefent Year.

I. The

I. The beſt, if not the only way, to print a good Edition of any antient Book, is to examine with Care the *written* Copies of it. And the Text of antient Books is allowed by the Learned to be more or leſs perfect, as more or fewer MSS have been collated for that Purpoſe. For this reaſon, almoſt all *the Greek MSS of the New Teſtament*, which are now extant, *have been examined, and their Variations publiſhed*; greatly to the ſatisfaction of all thoſe, who are Friends to Religion and Learning.

II. The ſame Advantage, ariſing from a Colla-tion of MSS, to which antient Books are naturally entitled, has been readily granted to them all; except, perhaps, in the ſingle caſe of *the Hebrew Bible :* which however, on many accounts, may require it more than any other book of Antiquity. For the *older* any Writings are, and the *oftner* they have been tranſcribed; the more Miſtakes have probably been made by the Tranſcribers. And it is certain, that the Books of the Old Teſtament are, at leaſt ſome of them, the oldeſt in the world; and, that they have all been tranſcribed very fre-quently. As ſeveral of the Hebrew Letters are *very ſimilar*; it muſt have been the more eaſy for Tranſcribers to make Miſtakes. And the Miſtake of any one Hebrew Letter will often occaſion a very wide difference in the Senſe.

III. The Hebrew Copies, which have been hitherto printed, are found to agree with the *lateſt* and the *worſt* MSS. And the older the MSS are,

C the

the more they differ from the printed Text; for they generally read more agreeably to the Context, and also to the antient Versions. But farther; the Hebrew MSS will not only furnish many Various Readings, which make the Sense clear and consistent, where the printed copies are unintelligible or contradictory; but they will also vindicate *the Apostolical Quotations*. For some of the passages in the New Testament, quoted from the Old, which do not agree with the printed Hebrew Text, perfectly agree with the present MSS — particularly, in one important Prophecy, no less than 28 out of 32 MSS confirm a Quotation made by *St Peter* and *St Paul*; and this in a case, where the Reading, as *printed* in the Heb. Text by Masoretic Authority, invalidates the Reasoning of both these Apostles.

IV. The Hebrew MSS will not only correct many of the Mistakes, which have been introduced for 800 or 1000 years last past; but they will also confirm the Authorities of the *Greek, Syriac,* and the other antient and venerable Versions; which (under proper restrictions) will discover other Mistakes, made as early as the time of C h r i s t.

V. There are already known between 400 and 500 Hebrew MSS, now extant in different Parts of the World : of which number E n g l a n d contains more than any other Country; there being preserved at least *One Hundred and Ten* (containing the Whole or Parts of the Hebrew Bible) in the Universities of O x f o r d and C a m b r i d g e, and in T h e B r i t i s h M u s e u m. And since our

own Country is fo particularly happy in the Trea-
fure of its MSS, collected and brought hither at
an immenfe Expence ; it muft be honourable to
fet the Example *here*, in firft publifhing a Work
— which, tho' greatly defired by the Learned in
all Nations, has not yet been performed in any.

VI. In the CX MSS beforementioned are included 7 Copies of *the Samaritan Pentateuch*. And
as the only Copy of this Pentateuch hitherto publifhed (which was printed from a MS preferved in
France) has many very valuable Readings, where
the Hebrew Text is corrupted ; fo the 7 Samaritan
MSS, preferved in *England*, will correct fome confiderable Corruptions in the Samaritan Text, as it
is now printed from the *French* MS.

VII. Since thefe Hebrew and Samaritan MSS
are found to contain a great number of Various
Readings, though they have as yet been very im-
perfectly examined ; the Queftion, humbly propofed, is — Whether it muft not be the ardent
Wifh of every true Friend to Divine Revelation,
that *the Hebrew Text may no longer be deprived of an
Advantage, granted to all other antient Books* ; but,
that *its MSS may be examined, and their Various
Readings publifhed :* that fo the Miftakes, introduced by Tranfcribers, may be removed ; at leaft,
that nothing in our power may be wanting to render that Sacred Volume as nearly perfect, as Care
and Criticifm can now render it.

VIII. It muft be added : that, as many parts
of the prefent MSS are already obliterated by Age,

and others are conftantly decaying; the Various Readings in the parts yet legible ought to be collected without farther delay. And when the Various Readings fhall be publifhed; they will form a fafe and authentic Record; which (tho' the MSS fhould entirely perifh) will be always ready, either to reform the Hebrew Text, or correct our own Verfion.

IX. The Reafonablenefs therefore, or rather the Neceffity, of collating MSS being readily allowed, in order to procure an authentic Text of *all other* antient Writings; and a Collation of *the Greek MSS of the New Teftament* having been made, and juftly approved of: 'tis prefumed, that a Collation of *the Hebrew MSS of the Old Teftament* has been hitherto neglected, chiefly, on thefe two accounts — becaufe it was fuppofed, that *there were few Hebrew MSS now extant*; and, that *thefe few MSS contained very few if any Various Readings, and none of real Importance.*

X. To the number of above *Four Hundred* Hebrew MSS, before enumerated, there may be now added *many* others. For, tho' *one* only has lately been added to thofe found in *England*, which MS is preferved in the Cathedral Library at *Wells*; yet fuch has been the Zeal of feveral Englifh Proteftant Gentlemen in other Countries, particularly in *Italy*, that many Hebrew MSS (not publicly known) have already been difcovered, and more will probably be difcovered foon, thro' the indefatigable Endeavours of the Gentlemen beforementioned:

tioned : in which Enquiries they have been moft readily and zealoufly affifted by feveral Perfons of great Character and Diftinction in *the Church of Rome*. The chief Places, where fuch Enquiries have been, and are ftill making, are *Rome*, *Florence*, *Bologna*, *Milan*, *Genoa*, *Venice*, and *Conftantinople*.

XI. At ROME (not to particularize the Catalogues there obtained from other Libraries) a Catalogue has been lately publifhed of the Hebrew MSS in the THE VATICAN; in which grand Repofitory are preferved *Forty One* MSS of the Whole, or Parts, of the Hebrew Bible. And as Leave for collating any or all of thefe MSS, for the benefit of this Work, has been offered in the moft obliging manner by His Eminence CARDINAL PASSIONEI, who fo honourably prefides over The *Vatican* Library; the Offer has been thankfully accepted : and a Collation is now making of fome of the moft valuable, at the Expence of *Mr Kennicott*. And he has reafon to prefume, that his Work will be greatly enriched by the Various Readings of thefe excellent MSS; collated with great Accuracy, in the very Palace, and under the immediate Infpection, of *His Eminence Himfelf*. This Undertaking is alfo highly honoured by the Patronage of his Eminence CARDINAL SPINELLI; who has been pleafed to exert his Influence in favour of it at *Naples*, and alfo in other places.

XII. It has already been obferved, that the Various Readings in the Hebrew MSS are numerous;
. and

and particular Proofs have been selected. But abundant Demonstration of this point may *now* be given; in consequence of a regular and minute Examination made in *Three* of the oldest Hebrew MSS in *England*. As for instance: the Variations from the printed Text, which have been found in *One* MS of the *Pentateuch* (one of the oldest and best MSS now known) exceed Two Thousand; many of which considerably affect the Sense, and are consonant to the antient Versions: and (which furnishes a new and strong argument in favour of the *Samaritan* Text) there are in this one Hebrew MS not less than Seven Hundred Words, which differ from the printed *Hebrew*, but agree with the printed *Samaritan* Pentateuch.

XIII. Should it be enquired, Whether there be in *any other* antient MS a number of Variations at all proportionable, in *other* parts of the Old Testament; it may be answered, that in another MS (also one of the most antient and valuable now known) there are, in the Evangelical Prophet *Isaiah*, above One Thousand Readings different from the printed Text: and of these several have a considerable influence upon the Sense. So that the subjoining These, and all other Various Readings which may be found, at the bottom of every Page, in a new Edition of the Hebrew Bible, printed (*not with a new Text*, but) from one of the best Editions already published, must be a thing greatly desireable to all those, who would judge properly of the genuine Sense of the Old Testament.

XIV. If therefore Hebrew MSS, efpecially the more antient, do in fact contain numerous and important Variations from the Text, as it has hitherto been printed agreeably to the lateft MSS; and if the Various Readings, collected, will certainly be more numerous, and may alfo be more important, in proportion as more Hebrew MSS fhall be collated: it is humbly fubmitted, and muft be left to all thofe Societies, and to all thofe particular Perfons, who approve this Undertaking, to determine — *Whether this Work fhall be more, or lefs, perfect* ; by their enabling the perfon, undertaking it, to procure Collations of a greater or lefs number of the MSS abroad ; and alfo by enabling him to employ more or fewer Affiftants, for expediting the Work at home.

XV. Laftly : All thofe, who may incline to favour and patronize the prefent Undertaking, will pleafe to confider — that no Obligation is laid upon Subfcribers for the Continuance of their Subfcriptions — that the Subfcriptions will be defired no longer than a proper Progrefs fhall be made in the Work — and that, if fuch a Progrefs be made, there will be then (according to the method propofed by *The Delegates of the Prefs* in the Univerfity of O x f o r d) a Certificate given, at the end of every future year, as there is at the end of the prefent, by *The Royal Profeffor of Hebrew.*

O x f o r d ; *December* 18, 1760.

ACCOUNT II.

At the End of the Year 1761.

THIS Work being of a public nature, and having been honoured with very uncommon Encouragement; it feems neceffary, at the clofe of every year, to lay before the SUBSCRIBERS fome account of *the Progrefs made in the Work*, and alfo the State of *the Subfcription*. The proper notices, relative to both thefe particulars, are here communicated to my Patrons, at the conclufion of the *fecond* Year: and I beg leave to exprefs my warmeft gratitude, for the extraordinary Favour vouchfafed to my Undertaking by fo many SOCIETIES, and fo many PERSONS, who are themfelves eminently diftinguifhed, as well by their zeal for Religion and Learning, as by their Rank and Station. In particular, I think myfelf indifpenfably bound to make the moft dutiful, and moft humble, acknowledgment of A PATRONAGE, too important to be concealed, and too great to be fufficiently celebrated; which, to the extreme Honour of this Work, has been moft gracioufly extended to it by the Piety and Munificence of HIS MAJESTY.

The

The *Expediency* of fuch an Undertaking muft be evident to all thofe, who will attend to the following particulars —— that the defign of it is to do the fame juftice to the Text of the *Old* Teftament, which has been done (with univerfal applaufe) to the Text of the *New* Teftament, and to that of almoft all other antient writings —— that the Hebrew Text, tho' of fuch great importance, has been hitherto printed agreeably to the *lateft* and *worft* MSS —— that there are as yet happily preferved multitudes of *older* MSS; free from many of thofe later Corruptions, which difgrace that extenfive part of Divine Revelation: and MSS, which contain readings more agreeable to the *Context*, to the *Antient Verfions*, and alfo to the *New Teftament* —— and therefore, that it muft be exceedingly defireable, that as many as poffible of the Various Readings in thefe valuable MSS (now perifhing by age) be fpeedily collected; and afterwards accurately publifhed together (at the bottom of every page, in a new edition of the prefent Hebrew Text) for the information of the Learned, and the benefit of the Public. Thus much may be fufficient to be obferved here, as to the *Expediency* of this Undertaking; efpecially, after the fanction it has received from the united fuffrages of Learned Men thro' *Europe*.

As to the Hebrew MSS in *England*; the account, printed at the end of laft year, fet forth, that *One Hundred and Ten* had been then difcovered in this

D   Country.

Country. *Two* more have been since found in the public Libraries of *Oxford*. There is *One*, belonging to *Edward Wortley Montague* Esq; who has obligingly permitted it to be collated. *One* valuable MS has been purchased by myself. But the most considerable acquisition, during this year in *England*, consists in *Two* MSS, preserved in the Library of the Collegiate Church of *Westminster*. *One* Hebrew MS has been also discovered in the Library of *Marischal College*, *Aberdeen*: and *Two*, in that of *Trinity College*, *Dublin*; which were brought a few years since from *Africa* —— as appears from the account most obligingly procured by *The Right Honourable Lord Viscount* B E A U C H A M P.

The Collation of the MSS, in *England*, has been hitherto appropriated to the MSS in *Oxford*; in which University are preserved the greatest number, and some very antient and valuable. And the Work has been here carried on, with all the expedition consistent with health and exactness: the person undertaking it having been assisted in it constantly by *three* Gentlemen, and during part of the year by *four*.

The Various Readings, which have been discovered in this year's examination, are surprizingly numerous. Many of them are plainly of moment: but the merit of far the greatest part cannot be properly judged of, without much critical Examination; for which there is no leisure, during the progress of the Collation itself.

Ten

Ten MSS, containing parts of the Hebrew Bible, have been compleatly collated this year; and also parts of *Two* other MSS. And as the Collations of these *Twelve* MSS have been fairly transcribed, and those Transcripts have been carefully examined; the Original Collations are now deposited in the *Bodleian* Library, under the *Librarian's Seal* and *my own*: agreeably to the method prescribed by *The Delegates of the Press*, in their Order for a Subscription to this Work. It must be observed upon this article, that to the preceding MSS may be added (*as being collated likewise in the present year*) all such, as have been collated for this Work in *foreign* Countries.

For, whilst diligent attention has been employed on this Work at home; constant endeavours have been used to procure assistance from abroad : and indeed these endeavours have been attended with such Success, as cannot perhaps be paralleled on any other literary occasion. Great zeal has been shewn in favour of it, in many Countries very distant from *England*, and from one another; and by Learned Men of very different persuasions in Religion, who have united in their opinions of *the tendency of this Work to promote* (the common cause) *the Honour of Revelation*; and who have been very obliging by the assistance already granted, and by the kind offers of farther services.

As many valuable Hebrew MSS are preserved in the *Vatican* Library; leave for collating any, or all, of them was voluntarily offered by the late learned Librarian, the juftly-eminent Cardinal PASSIONEI: who conferred on the undertaker of this Work fignal obligations, by the honour both of his Patronage and his Correfpondence. The lofs of fo great a Friend has been very benevolently compenfated by the Patronage and Correfpondence of his Eminence Cardinal SPINELLI, *Dean and Superior of the College of Cardinals*; who has condefcended to exert his extenfive influence, in favour of this Work; and was lately pleafed to offer *his Letters in recommendation of it to any part of the World.* It muft alfo be gratefully obferved, that his Eminence Cardinal ALBANI, the prefent Librarian, protects and countenances this Work at the *Vatican*; and has kindly favoured it with feveral recommendatory Letters; particularly, to *Marfhal* BOTTA ADORNO, Governor of *Tufcany*, and to *Count* FIRMIAN, the Imperial Secretary of State at *Milan.*

The Collation of the Hebrew MSS, agreed for at the *Vatican*, at the expence of 200 £, is now finifhed by the learned Profeffor *Conftanzi*; and the Various Readings of the MSS there collated (which have been found numerous and in feveral inftances important) are expected foon in *England*. But ftill, there are many other curious MSS in *Rome*: and the Collation of *fome* of thefe alfo will (at *my* requeft and expence) be foon undertaken.

I have alfo obtained leave, at *Florence*, to felect feveral Hebrew MSS, in the Imperial Library;

and thefe are now collating by the learned *Signior Bartoli*, and *Il Padre Berretta Vallombrofano*. This Collation is carrying on, by the favour of *Marfhal* B O T T A, under the Patronage of *Sir* H O R A T I O M A N N, His Majefty's Refident there; who has honoured this Work with his Recommendation, particularly to *Count* F I R M I A N. Great acknowledgments are alfo due to *Count* F I R M I A N himfelf, for the zeal he has expreffed in favour of this Work; which will probably receive great affiftance from the learned Imperial Profeffor *Henrico á Porta*, to whofe care his Excellency has particularly recommended it.

At *Hamburgh*, there are many Hebrew MSS, preferved in the public Library. And an agreement has lately been made with the learned Profeffor *Reimar*; who is now employed in collating *Seven* of the moft antient and valuable.

Several very valuable MSS being preferved in the Royal Library at *Turin*; application for leave to collate them was made fome time fince to the Sardinian Ambaffador at this Court by *The Right Honourable the Earl of* B U T E, *One of His Majefty's Principal Secretaries of State*: whofe Patronage of this Work is moft gratefully acknowledged. And I think myfelf obliged to exprefs my moft humble thankfulnefs for the great Honour done this Work by *His Majefty* T H E   K I N G   O F   S A R D I N I A, and *His Royal Highnefs the* D U K E *of* S A V O Y, who have gracioufly declared Themfelves *Patrons* of it. His Majefty hath condefcended to order, that all the Hebrew MSS in his States fhall be examined upon this occafion; and hath been pleafed to appoint Two Hebrew Profeffors to collate the moft valuable. Thefe notices I have received in a moft obliging Letter from Mr Dutens, the Britifh Refident at *Turin*.

In *Spain* (whilft enquiries are making as to the *Efcurial*, and other public Libraries) it muft be obferved, that about *Twenty* Hebrew MSS are preferved in the Library of the learned and reverend *Francifco Perez Bayer*, Canon and Treafurer of the great Church at *Toledo:* who has expreffed his readinefs to permit a Collation of them to be made, for the advantage of this Work.

Two valuable MSS have been very lately fent to *Oxford*, from *Rotterdam*, by *Mr Penfionary Meerman*; to whom this Work will probably be much indebted for the affiftance derived from thefe MSS, thus obligingly lent for its benefit. The fame great Favour has alfo been granted, with the utmoft readinefs, by the Univerfity of *Aberdeen*, at the requeft of their Noble Chancellor; and they have lately fent to *Oxford* the very elegant and valuable MS, preferved in their public Library.

As to the parts of *Europe* not before-mentioned, in which there have been alfo enquiries made after Hebrew MSS, during the prefent year; it may be proper to mention *Conftantinople*, *Warfaw*, *Venice*, *Naples*, *Bologna*, *Mantua*, *Pavia*, *Genoa*, *Lifbon*, *Geneva*, *Utrecht*, *Erfurth*, *Berlin*, and *Stockholm*. And amongft thofe Gentlemen, who have very

obligingly aſſiſted in theſe ſeveral enquiries, parti-
cular Thanks are due to their Excellencies *Lord
Viſcount* STORMONT, *Sir* JAMES GRAY, *the
Hon.* EDWARD HAY *Eſq*; and JAMES PORTER
Eſq; His Majeſty's Ambaſſadors and Envoys at
Warſaw, Naples, Liſbon, and *Conſtantinople.*

To theſe various inſtances of extraordinary Service ſo zealouſly granted to this Work, and of
Honour thus unexpectedly conferred upon the undertaker of it, muſt be added the great Favour
already ſhewn, and the extenſive Aſſiſtance likely
to be granted, by the Learned at *Paris.* In particular, the moſt grateful acknowledgments muſt
be here made to *Monſieur L'Abbé* LADVOCAT,
the very worthy Librarian and Hebrew Profeſſor
at *the Sorbonne*; who propoſes to employ himſelf,
together with ſome able Aſſiſtants, in collating for
this Work ſeveral very valuable MSS.

Such is the State, at preſent, of this Collation.
And from the preceding account of the Work,
compared with the ſubſequent liſt of the Subſcribers, the Reader will be led to conſider ―― that
the Subſcription is fully ſufficient to ſupport and
encourage a diligent Collation of the MSS in
England, and to procure conſiderable Aſſiſtance
from other Countries ―― but that this Work will
certainly be the more perfect, in proportion as a
greater number of valuable MSS ſhall be collated
abroad : of which there are happily found ſo very
many, and leave is with ſo much public ſpirit

granted for the ufe of them, in the various parts of *Europe*. The Public may be affured, that I fhall continue to exert my utmoft endeavours, in proportion to the encouragement I receive, towards perfecting of the Work, in which I have the honour to be thus employed. And I beg leave to hope, that neither the preceding narrative, nor the following lift, will by any means be interpreted as matter of oftentation. I have only given a plain enumeration of the great Favours in fact conferred by others, adding fome expreffions of my own gratitude. And it may be prefumed, that fuch an Account will be agreeable to all *the fincere Friends* of this Work —— and T H E S E are the Readers, whom I am ftudious and ambitious to pleafe.

Laftly: All thofe, who may be inclined to favour and patronize the prefent Undertaking, will pleafe to confider —— that no Obligation is laid upon Subfcribers for the continuance of their Subfcriptions —— that the Subfcriptions will be defired, no longer than a proper Progrefs fhall be made in the Work —— and that, if fuch a Progrefs be made, there will be then (according to the method propofed by *The Delegates of the Prefs* in the Univerfity of O x f o r d) a Certificate given at the end of every future Year, as there is at the end of the prefent, by *The Royal Profeffor of Hebrew*.

O x f o r d ; *Dec.* 16, 1761.

THE CERTIFICATE.

THE Delegates of the Press, in the University of Oxford, having in January 1760 subscribed to Mr Kennicott's Collation of the Hebrew MSS; and having inserted in an Order then made the following words [*That their Subscription be continued at the beginning of every Year, upon Mr Kennicott's producing a Certificate from the Royal Professor of Hebrew, that in his Judgment Mr Kennicott hath made a competent Progress in the said Work during the Year preceding* ;] and Mr Kennicott having applied to me for such a Certificate : I do hereby accordingly Certify, for the Satisfaction of the said Delegates, and of such other Persons as have encouraged this Work by their Subscriptions, that the several Parts of the Collation (made during this Second Year) have been laid before me. And my Opinion is, that Mr Kennicott hath made a very competent Progress in the said Collation, and indeed advanced farther in it than could have been reasonably expected ; considering the extensive Correspondence he has established, in several Parts of Europe, for the greater Perfection of this Undertaking. And, upon considering several of the Various Readings, which he has already discovered in the Hebrew MSS ; I think this Work will be of very considerable Service to Sacred Literature.

THO. HUNT,

Chris-Church ;
Decemb. 7, 1761.

Regius Professor of Hebrew.

E

THOUGH I have finished the Account of the *Second* Year; excepting the List of the SUBSCRIBERS, who are reserved for one compleat enumeration, at the conclusion of the whole Narrative: I shall not begin the Account of the *Third* Year, till I have previously inserted one material particular, which seems to be here necessary.

The Work having been described, as going on both at home and abroad; it is probable, that the curious Reader has already wished to know —— *Upon what Plan the Collation itself was conducted.* I shall therefore state here the mode of proceeding; so as to convey some idea, both of the *Labour* which was requisite, and of the *Exactness* which was aimed at.

As to the LABOUR: tho' every work, which demands close attention for many hours in a day, must be thought laborious; yet what an idea would the Reader form of the pity due to himself, were he to repeat, over and over, *the Letters* of the Alphabet, only varied in their order and connexion, for no longer a time than three hours in a day, during one month! I say, were he to repeat *the Letters*; because this was of necessity the rule to be followed in the case before us. For, according to the general pronunciation of Hebrew words, some Letters are not sounded; and if, upon such a plan, the reading had been *by whole words,* very numerous would have been the mistakes. And if a system a fyftem of pronunciation had been invented, which could exprefs diftinctly every Letter in every Word; yet even then reading *letter after letter* was certainly a more fure method, tho' more flow and more laborious. When the Reader has ruminated, for a few minutes, on the fatigue of naming in a printed copy, and examining in a MS, letter after letter, thro' a fingle chapter containing but 20 or 30 verfes; he is only requefted to add to the former idea that of the number of verfes in the whole Old Teftament: which amount to *Twenty Three Thoufand, One Hundred, Eighty Five.*

As to the other article, that of EXACTNESS; which indeed is of the utmoft moment in Such an Undertaking: that the learned Reader may judge, how far this grand point was likely to be fecured by the feveral rules formed for this purpofe, I fhall infert here a copy of *The Method*, which I eftablifhed at home, and which I fent to thofe who collated for me in other parts of Europe.

METHODUS

VARIAS LECTIONES notandi, et res fcitu neceffarias defcribendi, a fingulis Hebraicorum Codicum MStorum Veteris Teftamenti Collatoribus, (a LECTORE fcilicet atque SCRIPTORE) obfervanda.

COLLATOR quifque, qui hanc fufcipit et ornare vult provinciam, fibi accerfet fidum laboris focium; et, focio legente codicem impreffum, ipfe infpiciet codicem MStum, defcribetque

E 2 difcre-

difcrepantias. Editio impreffa, quæ eligitur, eft
illa a *Van der Hooght* edita, *Amftel.* 2 *tom.* 8°. 1705.
Et modus, quo legitur codex hic impreffus, non eft,
fingula recitando verba, vel (ut aiunt) *verbatim,*
fed (prout res hæc omnino poftulat) *literatim,* feu
fingulas recitando literas.

In codice MSto perlegendo notandæ funt om-
nigenæ, quotquot funt, Verborum et Literarum
(non punctorum vel accentuum) a codice impreffo
diverfitates : five fint 1°. *Additiones* ; 2°. *Omiffiones* ;
3°. *Tranfpofitiones* ; 4°. *Variationes* ; 5°. *Correctiones* ;
6°. *Refuræ.* Hæ fex diverfitatum fpecies notandæ
funt (non quòd harum fingula fit per fe colligenda,
et feorfim a cæteris notanda, fed notandæ funt
diverfitates promifcuè, atque eo quo inter conferendum occurrunt ordine) fuper chartæ paginam
duas in columnas divifam ; quarum finiftra continet verba codicis impreffi, cum libro Biblico fuprapofito ; dextera verò continet diverfitates codicis
MSti, fuprapofito MSti titulo : fequuntur exempla.

ADDITIONES.

2 *Samuel.*		MS. *Bodleian.* N°. *&c.*
23, 17	- - - - יהוה	- - - - - - מיהוה
— 4	- - - יורה שמיש	- - - - - - יורח יהוה שמש
Deuteron.		MS. *&c.*
28; 27, 28	- יכבה : להרפא	{ להרפא מכף רגלך ועד - - יכבה : קדקדך }
Pfalm.		MS. *&c.*
25, 17	tot. comma (*verfus*)	bis fcriptum, *vel* repetitum.

Si plurima addantur verba, non repetita, fed
diverfa a præcedentibus ; ea defcribantur omnia.

OMISSIONES.

Genes.	MS. &c.	
49, 10 - - - - שילה	- - - - - - -	שלה
Zachar.	MS. &c.	
14, 18 - - ולא עליהם	- - - - - -	עליהם
Ezek.	MS. &c.	
16, 6 ⎰ ואמר לך בדמיך חיי ⎱ ⎱ ואמר לך בדמיך חיי ⎰	- - ואמר לך בדמיך חיי -	
Malac.	MS. &c.	
2; 15, 16 ⎰ נעריך אל יבגד : ⎱ ⎱ כי שנא שלח ⎰	omissa.	

Si fuerint omissa in uno loco verba quamplurima,
fc. 20, 30 vel 40 ; exprimatur veroum *primum* et
ultimum fic omissum, atque fic fiat notatio :

Ezek.	MS. &c.
7 ab עליך (1°) in com. 4, ⎰ ad עיט inclusivè in com. 9 ⎱	omissi.

Ubicunque verba, vel ob vetuftatem, vel ob
paginam dilaceratam, legi non poffunt ; notandum
eft hoc modo : *verba a — ad — legi non poffunt* ;
vel *verba hæc —, paginâ dilaceratâ, defunt.*

TRANSPOSITIONES.

Ezek.	MS. &c.	
31, 8 - - - כפראתיו	- - - - - - -	כפארתיו
Amos.	MS. &c.	
8, 3 - - - ארני יהוה	- - - - - -	יהוה ארני
Job.	MS. &c.	
18, 4 - - - ויערק צור	- - - - - -	וצור יעתק
Num.	MS. &c.	
23, 1 ויאמר בלעם אל הלק	- - בלעם אל הלק	ויאמר בלק אל בלעם
Job.	MS. &c.	
21; 8 et 9 commata - -	tranfp.	

Si Scriptor, in defcribendâ variante aliquâ, hoc
erret modo —— verbum impref... in columnâ

dexterâ, et MStum in columnâ finiftrâ, perperam
fcribendo; errorem citiùs corriget et meliùs, non
verba delendo, fed lineam hujufmodi formando:

VARIATIONES.

	2 Sam.		MS. &c.
23, 18	- - - - השלישי	- - - - - - - השלשה
— 13	- - - שלשים	- - - - - - שלשה
	Jerem.		MS. &c.
50, 38	- - - ובא מים	- - - - - - ובה מים
	Ezek.		MS. &c.
13; 11, 12	- תבקעי: והנה	- - - - תבקעו: הנה
	1 Sam.		MS. &c.
20, 2	- - - - לו עשׂה	- - - - - - לא יעשׂה

Ubicunque initium verbi fcribitur in fine lineæ,
et aliter fcribitur initium ejufdem verbi in lineâ
fequenti; notandum, hoc modo:

	1 Chron.	MS. &c.
5, 6	- - - - פלנאסר	פלאס ‖ פל.אסר

Hìc quoque obfervare licet rem momenti haud
levis, et a Collatoribus (præcipuè a Lectore)
perpetuò curandam : fi bis, vel ter, vel quater,
occurrat in eodem commate verbum aliquod de-
fcribendum; fedulò notandum, an fit verbum id,
quod 1°, vel 2°, vel 3°, vel 4°, occurrit; hoc modo:

	Pfal.		MS. &c.
39, 6	- - - כל הבל כל	- - - - 1°. כל omiff.
	Ifai.		MS. &c.
52, 9	- - 2°. ירושלם	- - - - - - ישראל
	Jud.		MS. &c.
1, 27	- - 3°. בנותיה	- - - - - - בנתיה
	Ifai.		MS. &c.
40, 21	1°. 3°. 4°. — הלוא	- - - - - הלא
—	- - - 2°. — הלוא	- - - - : אם לא

CORRECTIONES.

Iſai.	MS. &c.
30, 4 - - - - - הנה	ם primò (a primâ manu) ם
Deuteron.	MS. &c.
25, 18 - - - - - אלהים	כ primò ך
1 *Reg.*	MS. &c.
14, 31 - - - - - אביה	ם primò ה
15, 2 - - - - - בת -	רת primò ן

Si verba vel literæ in MSto ita corrigantur, ut
prima ſcriptio clara adhuc ſit et *certa*; notandum
eſt — primò *ſic*. Si non certum ſit, ſed tantùm
probabile, quid primò ſcriptum fuit; notandum
eſt, quòd talis litera *hæc* vel *illa* fuiſſe *videtur*;
vel deſcribendum per particulam *fortaſsè*: ut, ב
fortaſsè primò כ — ד fortaſsè ר — ת fortaſsè ה vel
ה — ו fortaſsê י — ה fortaſsê ו &c.

RASURÆ.

Ezek.	MS. &c.
16, 57 - - - - - ארם	אֹרֶם —— ר primò ד
2 *Sam.*	MS. &c.
23, 5 - - - - - וישמרה	וישמרֶה —— ר primò ור ס
Jud.	MS. &c.
4, 13 - - - - - וייעק	חָוֶק —— unâ literâ eraſâ.
1 *Reg.*	MS. &c.
1, 24 - - - - נתן אדני	נתן אֲֹֹאדני 2 literis eraſis.
Iſai.	MS. &c.
41, 1 - - - - - יחרו	—— 3 lit. eraſis.
12 — וכאפס אנשי מלחמתך	ſcripta ſupra raſuram.
Pſal.	MS. &c.
47, 8 - - - - - כל	עֹל כל —— עֹל ferè eras.
Iſai.	MS. &c.
9, 5 -- נתן [בן]	3 vel 4 literæ, primò inter hæc verba ſcriptæ, e mediâ lineâ nunc ſunt ſcalpello exciſæ.

Si fint fupra rafuram *pauca* verba vel literæ, *ufitatæ* magnitudinis et diftantiæ ; notandum eft, quæ fint hæc verba vel literæ : et fi dentur fupra rafuram verba in uno loco *quamplurima* ; ita notentur :

Levit.	MS. *&c.*
8 a ויהגר 1°. in com. 7, ad את 2°. inclufivè in com. 9.	hæc 41 verba funt fupra rafuram.

Nota etiam adhibenda eft, ubi fupra rafuram verba vel literæ inufitatè *conftipantur* ; ibi etenim fcripta fuerunt primò *pauciora* verba vel literæ, quàm nunc fcribuntur. Et notandum denique, ubi fupra rafuram verba vel literæ a fe invicem inufitatè *diftant* ; ibi etenim fcripta fuerunt primò *plura* verba vel literæ, quàm nunc fcribuntur.

ALIA QUÆDAM IN

CODICIBUS HEBRAICIS V. T. CONFERENDIS

OBSERVANDA.

1. In literis a *Lectore* recitandis, fiat paufula quædam poft quodque verbum, vel faltem vocis variatio in ultimâ verbi literâ pronunciandâ ; ut fciat *Scriptor*, an ex tot literis conftet verbum in MSto, quot habet codex impreffus ; an non : e. g. an אשדת (*Deut.* 33, 2) vel שלהבתיה (*Cant.* 8, 6) vel ביתאל &c : (plurimis in locis) fcriptum fit quafi verbum unum, vel duo.

2. Lector cautè notum faciat, quotiefcunque fibi occurrit aliqua litera, quæ fit *majufcula* vel *minufcula,*

cula, *suspensa* vel *inversa* &c: ut caveat Scriptor, de hisce rectè admonitus. Caveat denique Lector, quando monet Scriptorem ad quod comma pertinet hoc vel illud verbum, ne erret hac de causâ, quòd datur aliquando triplex, sæpius duplex, commatum numerus in margine ejusdem lineæ: ex. gr. figuræ, quæ indicant commata 1, 2, 3, sunt in margine ejusdem lineæ, ad 1 *Chron.* 1, 1. Et quum in singulis capitibus editionis impressæ commata 5, 10, 15, 20, 25, 30, &c. numerantur, non *figuris* arithmeticis (ut cætera commata) sed *literis* Hebræis alphabeticis; eo major erit *Lectoris* cura in numeris horum commatum assignandis, quo facilius errare potest ob conjunctionem literarum in margine cum figuris.

3. Si verba ullibi, evanida præ ætate, atramentum de novo acceperint; cautissimè disquirendum est Scriptori, in verbis saltem majoris momenti, et in literis similibus, an non secunda manus intulit lectiones a primis diversas. Quod si fiat; notanda est prima lectio, ubicunque ab impressi codicis lectione differt. Addere licet: quòd Collator literas fere deletas, et minimos literarum apices, capiet meliùs et discernet; si vitro microscopico, pro re natâ, utatur.

4. Notandæ sunt, si modò occurrant in MSto insignes discrepantiæ, quoad *totos Libros:* ex. gr. si tres libri Poetici (*Psalm. Job.* et *Proverb.*) scripti sint more Poetico, in Hemistichiis; adeo ut dextera columna seriatìm habeat primas commatum partes, sinistra columna ultimas.

F 5. Notandæ

5. Notandæ funt infignes difcrepantiæ, quoad Capitum vel Pfalmorum *initia*: ex. gr. fi *Pfalmus* 43 (שׁפְּטֵנִי &c.) non quafi Pfalmus novus exordiatur, fed fequatur quafi pars *Pfalmi* 42 ; abfque fpatio vacuo, vel literis folito majoribus.

6. Notandæ funt voces, quæ (cæteris punctatis) manent *non punctatæ*; et voces, quæ *duo puncta* habent fupernè pofita : nec non et *voces imperfectæ*, vel *vocum partes*, quæ verarum lectionum fæpe funt veftigia : notandum quoque *fpatium* aliquod infigne, quod *in medio verfuum* alicubi invenitur.

7. Notandæ infuper variæ lectiones, quæ in *margine* MSti occurrunt ; fi modò non fint eædem, quæ nomine *Keri* jam funt fatis notæ : fi fint *Keri* vulgatæ, poffunt negligi. In vocibus, quæ habent *Keri* in margine, cautè videndum an non literæ in textu funt mutatæ ; et an non ipfum *Keri* fuit in textu a primâ manu.

8. Bene aget Scriptor, fi, inter codicem aliquem conferendum, initia capitum, et commata 10^m. 20^m. 30^m. &c, *penicillo* in margine notaverit : nam, hoc facto, facillimè invenientur loci, ad quos recurrendum erit Collatoribus, quum ad examen revocanda vel tranfcribenda fuerit MSti collàtio.

9. In omni MSto conferendo, notandum *quas* habeat *partes* Veteris Teftamenti, et qualis fit *ordo librorum* — Si codex habeat *puncta* ; et fi puncta videantur literis coæva — Si habeat, inter libros Pentateuchi, fpatium 3 vel 4 linearum, vel amplius fpatium — Si habeat *Maforam*, in fummâ et imâ

pagînâ,

paginâ, et in margine ; an non — Si voces librorum *initiales* fint majores et ornatæ, vel fimplices
et cæteris literis magnitudine prorfus æquales —
Notandum præcipuè, fi alicubi detur *tempus* five
annus, quo fcriptus fuit codex MStus ; quæ æra
fæpius occurrit in fine codicis, aliquando tamen
huic vel illi libro in medio codicis fubnexa eft : et
in verbis, quæ æram hanc exprimunt, defcriben-
dis, accuratè obfervandum, an non inter literas
numerales a fecundâ quadam manu inducta fuit
mutatio. Si vero nullibi occurrat, in codice fcriptus, ætatis fuæ annus ; eruditus tamen Collator
notabit, quòd codex *valde antiquus*, vel *non valde
antiquus*, effe videatur ; et quòd fæculo *decimo*,
undecimo, *duodecimo*, *decimo tertio*, vel *decimo quarto*
&c : haud immeritò fit adfcribendus.

Liceat denique exoptare, atque fpem fovere,
quòd Viri Eruditi, qui in variis Europæ partibus
Collationi huic operam vel dant, vel funt daturi,
facrum Opus fuum, non modò curâ fummâ, fed et
fide religiofiffimâ profequentur ; femper memores
hujus apud Rabbinos celeberrimæ fententiæ :

אין בתורה אפילו אות אחת
שאין הרים גדולים תלויין בה :

NON EST IN LEGE VEL UNA LITERA,

A QUA NON PENDENT MAGNI MONTES.

ACCOUNT III.

At the End of the Year 1762.

THIS Work &c.   *The Introduction to the Account, for this Year, is not given here; because it is nearly the same, as for the last Year: see pages* 24 *and* 25.

As to the Hebrew MSS in our own Country: the Account, printed at the end of the year 1761, specified *Nine*, which had not been before publicly taken notice of; and, by the addition of these to such as were before known, the whole number preserved in Great Britain and Ireland amounted to *One Hundred and Nineteen.* This ample and sacred Treasure, imported from various parts of the world, has lately been encreased by the arrival of another Hebrew MS, purchased at *Constantinople:* a MS, which was (with great difficulty) procured by JAMES PORTER *Esqr*, His Majesty's late Ambassador. And as His Excellency has been pleased, in the most obliging manner, to make me a Present of it; I think myself happy in this public opportunity of expressing my thanks for so great a favour. The whole number of these MSS is now become *One Hundred and Twenty One,* by the notice lately
received

received of a MS Bible, in the hands of *Mr Chalmers*, of *Auld-bar* in Scotland ; who brought it, fome years fince, from *Gibraltar*.

During the firft two years of this Work, the Collation (in England) was confined to the Hebrew MSS in O x f o r d ; in which Univerfity are preferved the greateft number, and fome very antient and valuable. But the laft year, which was the *Third*, was almoft entirely employed in collating the Hebrew MSS preferved in C a m - b r i d g e ; and thefe, tho' making *Nine* large volumes, have been completely collated within the year. And here I beg leave to exprefs my grateful acknowledgments to that Illuftrious Univerfity, for the fignal honour done me, in granting leave (by an unanimous Vote of their Senate) that I fhould take their MSS with me to Oxford : a favour, which has greatly contributed to the convenience, and ftill more to the expedition, with which they have been all collated. And yet, large as this fhare of the Work is ; there were alfo collated in the laft year *Two* Folio MSS, obligingly fent me from *Rotterdam* by the learned *Mr Penfionary* M e e r m a n.

To the preceding MSS muft be added, as collated likewife in the laft year, all fuch as have been collated, on this occafion, in *foreign* Countries. For, whilft diligent attention has been employed on this Work at home, and *Five* or *Six* Affiftants have been engaged in it, for the fake of greater

expe-

expedition; endeavours have been ufed to procure affiftance from abroad: and indeed thefe endeavours have been attended with fuch fuccefs, as cannot perhaps be paralleled on any other literary occafion. Great Zeal has been fhewn in favour of it, in many countries very diftant from England, and from one another; and by Learned Men of very different perfuafions in Religion; who have united in their opinions of the tendency of this Work to promote (the common caufe) *the Honour of Revelation:* and who have been very obliging by the Affiftance already granted, and by the kind offers of farther Services.

And here, as the many and great Patrons of this Work have a right to be fully acquainted with the Favour fhewn to it abroad; and as a few, who may not be kindly affected towards it, might otherwife fuggeft their doubts of the extraordinary Approbation of it amongft Learned Foreigners; I hope to confult the fatisfaction of the former, by inferting the two following articles. The *firft* is a copy of the Certificate, which was voluntarily fent me from R o m e by (my late honoured Patron there) *Cardinal* P a s s i o n e i, figned and fealed by his Eminence Himfelf: a Certificate, which is to be confidered as coming, not from a private perfon, but from One acting in fo high and public a character, as that of *Cardinal Librarian to the Roman Church.* The *fecond* is a copy of the Extract from the Public Regifter of the Univerfity of

G e n e v a;

GENEVA; which copy was moſt obligingly procured, and ſent to England, by *The Right Honourable Lord* MOUNT-STUART.

The *Certificate* from ROME.

*L' Entrepriſe d'une nouvelle Edition de la Bible, qui
doit ſe faire à Oxford ſur tous les Manuſcrits Hebraïques, qui peuvent ſe trouver dans les plus célèbres
Bibliotéques, a trouvée ici autant d'approbateurs, que de
perſonnes qui en ont entendû parler. Et pour favoriſer
les Auteurs d'un ſi important Ouvrage, j'ai permis avec
plaiſir la Collation des anciens Manuſcrits Hebraïques,
qui ſe trouvent dans la Bibliotéque Vaticane ; et je l'ai
accordée en qualité de Bibliotéquaire de la Ste. Egliſe Ro-
maine. A Rome ; ce ſeize May, mil ſept cent ſoixante
un.* D. Card^l. PASSIONEI,
                    Bibliot. de la S. E. R.

The *Certificate* from GENEVA.

*Extrait des Regitres de la Vénérable Compagnie des
Paſteurs et des Profeſſeurs de l' Egliſe de Genève.*

Du Vendredi, 4. Decembre, 1761.

*Monſr. le Recteur et Meſſrs. les Bibliothécaires ont
raporté, qu'on leur a fait part d'un Projet formé en
Angleterre, pour la Collation des Manuſcrits Hébreux de
l'Ancien Teſtament, & qu'on leur a demandé la commu-
nication de ceux que nous pourrions avoir dans notre Bibliothéque ; qu'il paroit par un Imprimé Latin, que le
principal exécuteur de ce Projet eſt Monſr. Benjamin
Kennicott Maitre ès Arts a Oxford ; Projet, par l' exécution du quel on ſe propoſe d' eclaircir à bien des*
                                                    égards

*égards le Texte Sacré, et d'en aplanir les difficultez ; que
pour parvenir à ce but l'Autheur avoit deja pris des
mesures our puiser dans les principales Bibliothéques de
l'Europe, et qu'il avoit des assurances qu'elles lui seroient
ouvertes. Sur quoi opiné, la V. Compagnie a reconnu una-
nimement toute l'utilité, qui peut resulter de l'exécution
de ce Projet, et combien il importe de faire par raport
aux Livres de l'Ancien Testament ce qu'on a deja fait
avec succez à l'egard de ceux du Nouveau. Elle n'a pu
qu'aplaudir aux louables intentions du l'Autheur, et de
ceux qui s'interessent a la perfection d'un Ouvrage, dont
on a lieu d'esperer de grands avantages pour une plus
parfaite intelligence des Livres Sacrez, et par cela
même pour la Religion ; et elle est persuadée que cette
Entreprise, qui fait beaucoup d'honneur au zéle de son
Autheur, sera généralement aprouvée. En conséquence
Messrs. les Bibliothécaires ont été chargez de communiquer
ce qu'il pouroit y avoir dans notre Bibliothéque de relatif
à cet object.   Du Vendredi, xi. Decembre, 1761.*

*Monsr. le Recteur a demandé la permission de com-
muniquer Copie de le Delibération ci-dessus à Milord
Mount Stuart, qui l'a desiré.   Accordé.*

BUISSON, *Secretaire.*

In the last Annual Account of this Work, notice was given, that the Collation of the Hebrew
MSS, agreed for at the *Vatican* at the expence of
200 £, was then finished. The Box, containing
this Collation, arrived safe about the middle of last
year ; and was delivered into my hand, without
the least expence for carriage : which I mention,

in

in grateful remembrance of the generofity of *Mr*
PAUL GAUSSEN, *Banker* at Geneva. The care,
with which this Collation feems to have been executed by Profeffor *Conftanzi*, has encouraged me
to fend a Commiffion for feveral other MSS; the
Collation of which will amount to nearly the fame
large Sum with the former.

There can be no doubt, but the Profeffor will
readily be admitted to this fecond Work; in confequence of the very honourable Patronage granted
me by His Eminence Cardinal SPINELLI, *Dean
and Superior of the College of Cardinals*: to whom I
am fignally obliged, for His application to the
NUNTIO at *Madrid*, and alfo to the Minifter from
HIS CATHOLIC MAJESTY at *Rome*, in order
to procure catalogues of the Hebrew MSS, preferved in the *Efcurial* and other public Libraries in
SPAIN. It is alfo gratefully acknowledged, that
the prefent *Cardinal Librarian*, His Eminence
Cardinal ALBANI, has condefcended to affure
me by Letter, that the Work fhall receive from
Him all the Encouragement in his power: His
Eminence has been alfo pleafed to fend me a catalogue of all the MSS of the Bible, in the Pontifical
Univerfity of BOLOGNA. The Work has the
honour likewife to be favoured by His Eminence
Cardinal TORREGIANI, *the Cardinal Secretary
of State*; who has very gracioufly offered His Affiftance, wherever it may be wanted. And laftly:
the two very learned Vatican Librarians, Monfign"

G   ASSE-

A s s e m a n i, who were fo obliging as to examine the laft Collation, and fend *a Certificate* (figned with both their Names) as to its *authenticity and exactnefs*, will be pleafed to accommodate the Collators as benevolently as they did before.

Notice was likewife given, that His Majesty The King of Sardinia had moft gracioufly appointed Two Profeffors, who were to collate (for the benefit of this Work) the valuable Heb. MSS preferved in the *Royal* Library at Turin. An excellent fpecimen of this Collation I received, laft September, from Profeffor *Pafini* ; together with a moft obliging Letter. And I have juft been favoured with a fecond Letter ; which gives an account, that the Profeffors have proceeded in this Work fo diligently, that they are now examining the *Sixth* of thefe Royal MSS.

At Florence, *Signior Bartoli* and *Il Padre Berretta Vallombrofano*, having finifhed the MSS at firft agreed for there ; I have fent a fecond Commiffion, for collating other MSS in the fame Imperial Library. The Various Readings of the firft Collation are expected daily ; as they were delivered, laft November, to the care of a Friend by His Excellency Sir Horatio Mann, His Majefty's Refident there : to whofe Goodnefs I am under many and great obligations. It muft alfo be obferved, that this Work was recommended by Sir Horatio Mann to His Excellency *Count* Firmian, Governor of the *Milanefe* ; and that the
learned

learned *Henrico A Porta*, the Imperial Hebrew Profeſſor at *Pavia*, who was commiſſioned by Count Firmian, has drawn up an account of the Hebrew MSS in the *Ambroſian* Library at M I L A N, and of every other MS in that Dutchy, which may be of any ſervice : and that the papers, containing theſe particulars, having been ſent ſome time ſince by Sir Horatio Mann, are every day expected. *

From *Geneva* I have been favoured, by Profeſſor *Vernet*, with an account of two valuable Hebrew MSS in the Library at Z U R I C H. Profeſſor *Breitinger*, who drew up that account, has made an offer of collating them ; which offer I have readily accepted, on the ſame proportion of Expence as at other places.

The Collation, which was ſaid in the laſt Account, to have been begun at H A M B U R G H, has been carried on with diligence by Profeſſor *Reimarus* ; from whom I have received two parcels of the Various Readings, which he has collected : and this very worthy Profeſſor is now engaged in proſecuting the remainder of the Collation, which is to be made in that city.

* —— *De tali tantoque Opere, laboriſſſimo utique ac ſumptuoſiſſimo, ad exitum perducendo, tractantes Angliæ Proceres, et Literati, laudem profecto eximiam promerentur : plurimumque commendandi etiam ſunt quotquot, ut idem perficiatur, amicam manum et opem adjungunt.* ——

Prof^r. *A Porta*, to Count *Firmian* ; *Sept.* 18. 1761.
G 2

From *Magdeburgh* I have been informed by my valuable Friend Mr *Sack*, first Chaplain to HIS MAJESTY THE KING OF PRUSSIA, that an examination of some of the BERLIN MSS has been undertaken by Professor *Schultz*, and Mr *Heinius* son of the celebrated Rector of the Royal Gymnasium; and that Professor *Murfinna* is collating one MS, called the *Codex Seidelianus*. I am also highly obliged to Mr *Sack*, for procuring me the use of a large parcel of MS Papers, containing Various Readings and Remarks on the Hebrew Text, drawn up by the late Dr *Jablonski*; whose name declares the value of his Papers.

As to PARIS: I am informed by my zealous Friend and Assistant *Monf. L'Abbé* LADVOCAT, that there are about *Thirty* Biblical Hebrew MSS in the Library of the *Sorbonne*, of which he is Hebrew Professor and Librarian. This justly-celebrated Professor has already collated several of these MSS, and proposes to collate several others, for the advantage of this Work. In the *Royal* Library, at Paris, are preserved near *Forty* Hebrew MSS; some of which are very valuable. And here I gratefully acknowledge my great obligation to His Excellency *The Duke De* NIVERNOIS; who, as He is a celebrated Patron of Literature, has been pleased to apply to *The Count de St.* FLORENTIN, Secretary to HIS MOST CHRISTIAN MAJESTY, in favour of this Work, with regard to these Royal MSS:

MSS: a circumftance, which I have the honour to mention, by His Excellency's permiffion.

To thefe various particulars it may be added, that enquiries have been made, and are ftill making, after Hebrew MSS, in other parts of Europe, and alfo in other parts of the World; in order to give to this Work as great a degree of perfection, as the nature of the Subfcription fhall admit. For, large as the Subfcription is, it will by no means be thought fo large, as to employ Learned Men, in all parts, to collate all the MSS that are worth collating. In proportion to the encouragement will be the completenefs of the Work; more or lefs perfect, as more or fewer Various Readings fhall be collected from antient MSS; and a greater or lefs number of thefe MSS will be confulted abroad, as there fhall be more or fewer Subfcribers to the Work. I fhall only add here, that no Perfon, who pleafes to fubfcribe, is at all obliged to continue his Subfcription; but he may withdraw his favour, as he grants it, at his pleafure.

Laftly: the Patrons of this Work may be affured, that, extenfive and laborious as it is, it will certainly be carried on with all the expedition poffible. And, as Thofe, who have a right to enquire, may be naturally defirous of knowing, WHEN *this Work will be completed*; I think it my duty to acquaint them —— that, tho' it be impoffible, as yet, to fix this period with any certainty, yet (if
it

it fhall pleafe G o d to continue my prefent Health)
the Collations in England will probably be finifhed
in *Seven* years from the prefent time —— and that,
when the MSS at home are collated (without wait-
ing for any farther affiftance from abroad) the
great Work will be then begun of preparing the
whole for the Prefs ; collecting from the many
feparate parcels the Various Readings relative to
each Chapter and Verfe ; referring, in every quotation of each MS, to that MS, by its proper
number ; and prefixing to the whole fuch *Prolegomena*, as may explain the nature of the Work,
defcribe the MSS made ufe of, and record with
gratitude the Names of All Thofe, who have patronized the prefent Undertaking.

O x f o r d ; *January* 15, 1763.

The C E R T I F I C A T E
from
The Royal Profeffor of Hebrew
nearly the fame as before :

fee page 33.

ACCOUNT IV.

At the End of the Year 1763.

THE Introductory Acknowledgment, with the Remarks on the Expediency of this Work, being nearly the same as before in pages 24 and 25, are not here repeated.

As to the Hebrew MSS, belonging to our own Country; their number was, in the laft annual account, *One Hundred and Twenty One.* To thefe I am now to add a compleat MS of the Old Teftament, written in *Syria* 657 years fince; which has been kindly purchafed for me, by the Rev. Mr *Mordaunt*, Chaplain to the late *Earl of* NORTHAMPTON, His Majefty's Ambaffador, at *Venice.* This, with two *Bodleian* MSS not before mentioned, (one containing the *Pentateuch* and the other the book of *Job*) make the number of Biblical Hebrew MSS, at prefent known in Great Britain and Ireland, *One Hundred and Twenty Four.* Of thefe there have been now collated *Thirty Two.* And the original Collations of *Eighteen,* having been fairly tranfcribed, are depofited in the *Bodleian* Library; agreeably to the method prefcribed by the Delegates of the Prefs, in their Order for a Subfcription to this Work.

Amongft

Amongſt other MSS, collated in this year, are *Six*, which belong to *The Britiſh Muſeum*. And here, the moſt grateful acknowledgments are made of the ſignal Honour done to this Work, and the undertaker of it, by the Trustees of that Muſeum. For at their general Meeting in February laſt, They were pleaſed to order, in conſequence of a Petition from me, moſt obligingly preſented by His Grace the Lord Arch-Biſhop of Canterbury — that *all their Hebrew MSS ſhould be taken with me to Oxford, and collated there*. And, out of their 26 MSS, 6 were accordingly delivered to me ſoon after; which will be returned, with care and fidelity, within the year.

One of theſe 6 MSS was the Samaritan Penta-teuch, given by Arch-Biſhop Uſher to Sir Robert Cotton; a copy, which is exceedingly valuable, being almoſt the only compleat one in Europe, uniformly written by the ſame hand: and it is above 400 years old. This, and a Bodleian MS of the ſame kind, have been collated with the Sama-ritan Text in the London Polyglott: and from this collation it appears, that the Samaritan Text in *that Polyglott* (in other reſpects worthy of great commendation) is very inaccurately printed; but that theſe 2 MSS will correct many of the Errors there found, and likewiſe ſeveral Errors found in the *Paris* Polyglott. And this is a point too im-portant to be paſſed over, without particular atten-tion, in juſtice to the Samaritan Pentateuch itſelf:

for

for it can be no wonder, that some very learned Men have judged it to be very erroneous; when that printed copy, on which such judgment has been (at least in England) generally formed, is found to be printed so incorrectly. But then, those MSS are deservedly to be held precious; which will greatly correct the printed Text of *that* Pentateuch, without the assistance of which the Hebrew Pentateuch (it is presumed) will never be restored to its original purity. In favour of this Pentateuch may be here added the remarkable testimony of Dr CUDWORTH, that Ornament to Learning and to our Country; who (in a treatise entitled *The Union of Christ and the Church*, translated by Mosheim) commenting on a Text, which is expressed in the printed Hebrew differently from the quotations of it in the New Testament, observes thus: *But lastly, that which is most of all considerable; altho' these Hebrew copies, which now we have, received from the Jews, read it otherwise; yet that incomparable antiquity of the* SAMARITAN *Pentateuch, which seems to be* TRUER IN MANY PLACES *than our copies are, hath it as it is four several times quoted in the New Testament.* To this authority may be added that of Sir ISAAC NEWTON; which is very favourable to a Collation of the Hebrew MSS, by asserting the corrupt state of the Text as printed: for I have lately seen, in that Great Man's handwriting, several Corrections of the printed Hebrew; some of which exactly coincide with the Corrections made by the learned Father *Houbigant.*

H   With

With thefe *Six* MSS, from the Britifh Mufeum, have been collated in this year *Four*, belonging to the Bodleian ; *Two*, lent from the library of the Dean and Chapter of Weftminfter ; *One*, very elegant and containing the whole Bible, fent me by the Univerfity of Aberdeen ; *Two*, from Trinity College, Dublin, which were obligingly brought and delivered to me by the Provoft himfelf ; and *One*, belonging to the Reverend *Hieronymus de Wilhem*, very kindly tranfmitted from *Lekkerkirk* near Rotterdam. For the ufe of all which MSS, I here exprefs my thanks, in the warmeft and moft grateful manner. In thefe 16 MSS have been found a great number of Various Readings, and feveral of confiderable confequence ; particularly, in the magnificent MS fent from *Lekkerkirk*. And in the Text of this MS is found the very word (fignifying ALL) in *Deuteron.* 27, 26 (printed in the *Samaritan* Text) which makes fo material a part of St Paul's quotation (*Galat.* 3, 10) and is fo necefſary to the Apoftle's argument, that our Englifh Tranflators have thought themfelves obliged to infert it, tho' it is not in the printed Hebrew. To this Lift of MSS, fome lent to me at home, and others fent to me from abroad, is to be added a very antient MS of the Hebrew Pentateuch, belonging to the learned Profeffor *Schultens* at Leyden ; which he has kindly promifed to fend me : and the Profeffor has alfo employed perfons, who are collating, under his own infpection (for the benefit of this Work) the MS of the Samaritan Pentateuch in the library at Leyden.

And here it is neceffary, that the PATRONS of this Work fhould be informed; that, to the MSS already enumerated, as collated during this year in England, muft be added many MSS collated in other Countries. For whilft diligent attention has been employed at home, all the endeavours poffible have been ufed to procure affiftance from abroad; and indeed thefe endeavours have been attended with fuch fuccefs, as cannot perhaps be paralleled on any other literary occafion. Great Zeal has been fhewn in favour of it, in many countries very diftant from England, and from one another; and by Learned Men of very different perfuafions in Religion; who have united in their opinions of the tendency of this Work to promote (the common caufe) *The Honour of Revelation*: and who have been very obliging by the Affiftance already granted, and by the kind offers of farther Services.

The Honourable Certificates from

ROME *and* GENEVA,

originally repeated in this Year's Account,

are here omitted;

not being here again neceffary.

See pages 47, 48.

In order that the feveral Collations, making abroad, may be carried on upon the fame plan, and with the fame attention to all the neceffary circum-

H 2   ftances,

ftances, which are obferved at home; a large Sheet, defcribing the whole Method, has lately been printed, and is fent to the Foreign Collators. *See pages 35 — 43.*

At R o m e: the great lofs, fuftained by the deaths of their Eminences the Cardinals P a s s i o- n e i and S p i n e l l i, is made up by the Patronage of their Eminences the Cardinals A l b a n i and T o r r e g i a n i: the latter, *The Cardinal Secretary of State*; the former, *The Cardinal Librarian* ⸺ and from Him I have had the Honour of being affured (in a moft obliging Letter fent me laft January) that *every Vatican MS, which I had mentioned, fhould be at the fervice of this Work.* With my grateful acknowledgments to their Eminences, I muft exprefs my thanks to the worthy Prelate *Monfigr.* M a r e f o s c h i, Secretary to the College *De Propaganda Fide,* for his countenance of this Work, and his many fervices to the Collator Pro- feffor *Conftanzi:* and alfo to the Reverend Fathers *Xavier Vafquez* and *Auguftino Giorgi,* of the *Auguf- tinian* Convent; to the College of the *Maronites*; and to Sig. Abbate *Ballarini,* librarian to Prince *Barbarini:* who have readily granted the ufe of their MSS, on this occafion. The 2d Commiffion, which I fent to Rome, was for the Collation of *Seventeen* MSS; *Twelve* in the Vatican, and *Five* in the other libraries before-mentioned: and the Pro- feffor, who has already collated fome of thefe MSS, has fent me the following notice ⸺ *In codicibus*

mox

mox laudatis, plures atque eas quidem magni momenti variantes lectiones me inveniſſe lætaberis; et, quod tibi gratiſſimum fore confido, in codice bibliothecæ Angelicæ ea Danielis et Eſdræ capita, quæ Chaldaice tantum ſcripta vulgo reperiuntur, tum Chaldaice tum etiam Ebraice ſcripta deprehendi. I cannot conclude this article, without expreſſing the very grateful ſenſe, which I have, of the many and great Obligations conferred upon me by *Daniel Creſpin Eſq*; my kind Correſpondent at Rome.

In S P A I N : a catalogue of the MSS of the Hebrew Bible, in the *Eſcurial*, was procured by the N U N T I O at *Madrid*, ſollicited by Cardinal Spinelli ; and was ſent me, a little before his Eminence's death. He had condeſcended to inform me, that he had earneſtly requeſted his Friend the Nuntio to procure catalogues of the Hebrew MSS, *quotquot vel in Regiis vel in publicis Hiſpaniarum bibliothecis eſſervantur* : and, as the Eſcurial catalogue was accompanied with a promiſe, that catalogues of the MSS in *the other public libraries* of Spain ſhould ſoon after be ſent likewiſe ; I ſhall ſtill hope to be favoured with ſuch other catalogues. I am alſo highly obliged to the learned and reverend F R A N C I S C O P E R E Z B A Y E R, Canon and Treaſurer of the great Church at Toledo ; who has favoured me with a very kind Letter, and an account of the ſeveral valuable Hebrew MSS in his own library : together with exact ſpecimens of the character, in which each MS is written : which ſpeci-

mens

mens are exceedingly elegant and curious. The
oldeft of his MSS was written in 1144.

Whether any of the MSS in Spain can be collated there; or whether the Favour will be granted
of fending a few of them at a time to England (as
hath been done from *Holland* &c :) is not yet certain. But confidering — that His Majefty THE
KING OF SPAIN has fhewn himfelf a Patron of
Learning, in feveral inftances — that I have been
honoured with affurances of the intention of His
Excellency the *Earl of* ROCHFORD, His Majefty's
Ambaffador, to apply to the Court of Spain upon
this occafion — and that application will be likewife made there, in favour of this Work, by *General* CRAUFURD, to whom I am already under
great obligations — there is reafon to hope for very
confiderable affiftance from that Country. And it
is particularly to be wifhed, that affiftance may be
derived from *that* Country ; which was fo remarkably inhabited by *Jews*, but a few centuries ago.

At TURIN: the Hebrew Profeffors, whom His
Majefty THE KING OF SARDINIA was pleafed to
appoint to collate the Royal MSS, having finifhed
the examination of *Six* (which were thought the
moft valuable) and having fairly tranfcribed their
Collations, will foon deliver them to the Britifh
Refident there, L. DUTENS Efq; from whom I
have juft been favoured with an obliging Letter,
affuring me of his readinefs to tranfmit them carefully to England.

At

At FLORENCE: a second Collation is carrying on by *Il Padre Berretta Vallombrosano & Signior Bartoli*; which confists of *Six* MSS: the former Collation, which was of *Four*, was finished, and very elegantly tranfcribed, laft year; and it was carefully fent by His Majefty's Refident there, his Excellency *Sir* HORATIO MANN; whofe Name I cannot mention, without expreffing my warmeft thanks for His Patronage of this Work, fhewn upon all occafions: particularly, for recommending this Undertaking to his Excellency *Count* FIRMIAN, Governor of the Milanefe — for applying to Him for a catalogue of the Hebrew MSS in the *Ambrofian* library at MILAN — for obtaining leave to have them collated — and procuring the learned *Henrico A Porta* to undertake the Collation of them. By this Profeffor an excellent account of thefe MSS was drawn up, at the defire of Count Firmian, and by Him fent to Sir Horatio Mann; at whofe requeft it was brought to England by His Grace *the Duke of* GRAFTON, who condefcended to take the charge of it. This Milan catalogue contains an account of *Fourteen* MSS, feveral of which feem very valuable; and one of them is the antient Samaritan Pentateuch, which *Montfaucon* wifhed to have collated. I have been favoured with a Letter from Profeffor *A Porta*, dated laft September; and he was then preparing to begin the Collation, which comprehends the whole *Fourteen* MSS.

At

At ZURICH: the collation of the two MSS in the public library, which Profeffor *Breittinger* had offered to undertake, has been deferred; leave to ufe thefe MSS not having been obtained from the Magiftrates of that Town. But it is hoped, that fuch leave is now obtained; application having been made to the Englifh Minifter refident at *Berne*, requefting him to defire it. And at BERNE there is an Hebrew MS, containing part of the Bible; which is foon to be collated, under the direction of Monf[r]. *Sinner*, the public librarian.

At HAMBURGH: the collation of the MSS has been fo far carried on by Profeffor *Reimarus*, that *three* antient MSS (containing together one whole Bible) have been examined; and their Various Readings are tranfmitted to me.

At BERLIN: the Reverend Mr *Sack*, firft Chaplain to His Majefty THE KING OF PRUSSIA, has fent me the Various Readings of the *Seidel* MS of the Pentateuch (preferved in the public library at *Halle* in Saxony) which has been collated by Profeffor *Murfinna*. And, amongft other obligations, which I am under to Mr *Sack*, for fervices done and notices fent, in relation to my Work, I am to thank him for the correfpondence of the learned Dr *Semler* at Halle.

At DRESDEN, in the Electoral library, is preferved a MS of the whole Hebrew Bible; the Collation

lation of which is carrying on, under the direction of Mr *Clodius* the librarian; for whose favour I am indebted to Mr *Raspe* His Majesty's librarian at Hanover. And at HESSE-CASSEL is an Hebrew MS, the merit of which is thought so considerable, that it has been the subject of a learned and useful Dissertation, published by Mr *Scheide*, in 1748: and I have therefore applied to my friend the celebrated Professor *Michaelis* at *Goettingen*; requesting his advice, as to the best method of procuring a good Collation of it.

The last place I have here to mention, in which MSS have been collated, and in which Collations are still making, for this Work, is PARIS: and it is no wonder there should be preserved in PARIS very many and very valuable MSS of the Hebrew Bible. I cannot but think myself therefore particularly happy, in finding there so able and so zealous a Friend to the Work, as M. *l'Abbé* LADVOCAT, Librarian and Hebrew Professor at the *Sorbonne*: a Gentleman, who has engaged to give up to this Collation part of his own time, as well as that of several of his Pupils, whom he has formed to this very business. In February last he sent me (elegantly transcribed) the Various Readings of *Seven* MSS of the Psalms. He has since collated *Nine* other Psalters; and some of their Variations (he acquaints me) are very important. In this undertaking of Professor *Ladvocat* there is one circumstance, which I think myself obliged to men-

I   tion;

tion; and I do it with particular gratitude — that, tho' he propofes to take to himfelf and his Pupils a great deal of Labour; neither He, nor They, will accept any pecuniary gratification. In the laft Letter, with which I was honoured by the Profeffor, he was pleafed to fay — *We have no fuch cuftom, in the Sorbonne; and we think ourfelves extremely happy, both my young people and myfelf, in being able to contribute to a Work fo ufeful, and even fo neceffary, to the ftudy of the Sacred Scriptures.*

Upon a review of the preceding particulars, I flatter myfelf that the PATRONS of this Work will be well fatisfied both at the progrefs which is made at home, and at the endeavours ftrenuoufly exerted to procure affiftance and information from abroad. As almoft every MS furnifhes fome material Variations; it muft be evident (at leaft to Men verfed in Criticifm and Claffic Literature) that in proportion, as more MSS, efpecially MSS of antiquity, are collated, the more ufeful muft this Work prove. There is not therefore any quarter of the World, from which I have not been, and am, ardently defirous to procure the knowledge and the ufe of Hebrew MSS: and accordingly think myfelf highly obliged for the difcovery of every MS of this kind. For this reafon I muft exprefs my thanks here to the learned Profeffor *Rau*, at Utrecht, and others; who have fent me notices of fuch MSS: and alfo to the Reverend Mr *Lind* (Chaplain to His Majefty's Ambaffador

at

at *Conftantinople*) and to every other Perfon, who is kindly making enquiries of the fame nature.

But however (large as the Subfcription is, and ample as the Edition of this Work will really be) it is not vainly pretended, that it will be poffible to procure collations of *Half* the Hebrew MSS, already known in *Europe* only. For even *That* will foon be pronounced impoffible ; when it is confidered, that the MSS of the whole or parts of the Hebrew Bible, which are *already known* (exclufive of thofe in our own Three Kingdoms) are — in *Italy*, 117 — *Germany*, 87 — *France*, 70 — *Holland*, 32 — *Spain*, 20 — *Swifferland, Denmark*, and *Sweden*, 10 — Total, already known abroad, 336. This fum, added to that of the MSS at home, amounts to 460 ; which will probably be extended to 500. And, how very defirable would it be ; if it were poffible to comprife in this Work the Various Readings of the whole *Five Hundred* MSS ! — if it were poffible to make it *at once* (excepting Errors in the Execution) *perfect in its kind* — without leaving *The Old Teftament*, after fo extenfive a Subfcription, ftill fubject to Appendix after Appendix, and Addition upon Addition ; as hath been the cafe with *The New Teftament*, and is the cafe at this very day. For there are yet many (perhaps an *Hundred*) MSS uncollated of this Second Part of Holy Scripture ; notwithftanding the 30 years labour of Dr *Mill*, who publifhed the Various Readings of near *One Hundred* MSS — tho' *Kufter* and

Bengelius

Bengelius have each added the Various Readings of *Twelve* other MSS — and tho' *Wetſtein* has made ample additions to all the former Editors.

In ſhort : all, that can be reaſonably expected, I may venture to aſſure the Public, ſhall be done. My beſt endeavours ſhall continue to be exerted for procuring Collations of as many MSS, and giving as great a degree of Perfection to this Work, as the nature of the Subſcription ſhall admit : and this, not only from a conviction of the Expediency and Importance of the Work itſelf (which is to me more and more clear, the farther the Work advances) but alſo from a juſt ſenſe of Honour, and under the due influence of Gratitude to T H O S E, who have with ſo much Public Spirit patronized the preſent Undertaking.

O X F O R D ; *December* 12, 1763.

The *C E R T I F I C A T E*
from
The Royal Profeſſor of Hebrew
nearly the ſame as before :
ſee page 33.

ACCOUNT V.

At the End of the Year 1764.

WHENEVER a Work, that is extensive and laborious in its nature, is undertaken in consequence of a Public Subscription; it must give pleasure to the Patrons, as well as to the Undertaker of every such Work, if it be found to advance with proper expedition, and likely to be compleated in a proper manner. *The Collation of the Hebrew MSS of the Old Testament*, as being attended with uncommon labour, and likely to prove of particular importance, has been distinguished by a more ample Subscription, and a more uniform Approbation thro' the several parts of Europe, than perhaps any other Literary Undertaking. And therefore, upon the present Occasion of addressing myself to the many Learned and Illustrious Patrons of it, at the conclusion of this Year, which is *The Fifth* from the beginning; I cannot conceal the Pleasure, which I feel in acquainting them, that the Work is now about HALF-FINISHED.

From the last Annual Account it appeared, that out of CXXIV MSS preserved in Great Britain and Ireland, there had been then collated XXXII;

and

and that the original Collations of XVIII, having been fairly tranfcribed, were then depofited in The Bodleian Library. During the prefent year there have been collated XVIII Hebrew MSS, and One MS of the Samar. Pentateuch: concerning which number, compared with other numbers, it may be proper to obferve, that a few MSS may contain larger parts of the Bible than many MSS; and yet, that the XIX MSS, collated in this year, contain above 116,000 Verfes. But this has by no means been the whole of the Work; for the Collations of XXVI MSS have been, in this year, fairly tranf-cribed: the Originals of which are depofited, with thofe of the XVIII tranfcribed before, in The Bodleian Library.

Of the XIX MSS, thus collated, VI were lent me (as the fame number had been laft year) from *The Britifh Mufeum*, in confequence of an Order moft obligingly made at a general Meeting of *The Truftees*: and thefe MSS are carefully returned. For the Ufe of III others I am highly obliged to *Oriel* and *Jefus* Colleges, in this Univerfity. And my thanks are due likewife to the very learned Pro-feffor *Schultens*; who fent me a curious MS, be-longing to his own Library at *Leyden*.

But, with refpect to Foreign Countries; my moft grateful Acknowledgments are to be made for the Honour of a Letter, which, at the command of His Majefty THE KING OF DENMARK, hath

been

been sent me by His Principal Secretary of State, His Excellency *The Baron De* BERNSTORFF. As this Letter furnishes a very striking instance of Royal Attention to Sacred Literature; as it expresses the Will and Pleasure of a Sovereign, who is celebrated through the World for having sent learned Men into Africa and Asia, for the noblest purposes; and as His Majesty's Pleasure has been signified in that Letter, in a manner exceedingly honourable to my Work; I here insert an exact copy of it. And I cannot doubt, but my Readers will see with great satisfaction this Royal Testimony, in favour of my Work, added to those other Testimonies which have been already communicated, and which are of too much consequence not to be still continued, in this Annual Narrative.

Reverend Sir,

The King being informed of the learned Work, which You are sparing no pains to accomplish viz. that of restoring by the help of Ancient Manuscripts the Original Text of the Divine Writings of the Old Testament; His Majesty thinks fit to assist You by all possible means, in order to promote a Design so truly useful to Religion and Learning, and consequently so much deserving the greatest Encomiums.

In this view I am honoured with His Royal Commands, to acquaint You, Sir, with the Arrival of some Ancient Copies of the Hebrew Bible lately purchased in Egypt for the Royal Library; and sent

hither

hither by some Gentlemen, who are actually making a Voyage in Arabia Felix, by His Majesty's Orders. You receive here inclosed a short account of the Condition of these valuable Remains of Antiquity. The King intends with Pleasure to give You leave to make Use of them. It depends only of You, Rev. Sir, to appoint some able Person here; who may examine, and, if You think it proper, collate these Manuscripts with printed Copies: in order to gather out of the former such Various Readings, as may occur therein. I hope, You will be persuaded beforehand, that the Person, employed by You to this purpose, will meet with all imaginable Readiness to facilitate his Task. And I beg, You will be sure of my best Wishes for the Success of your arduous Undertaking, that cannot fail to immortalize your Name; and, what to a Man of your religious way of thinking must be of infinitely more Value, will draw down upon You God Almighty's Blessing.

I am, with great Esteem and Sincerity,

Reverend Sir,

Your most obedient humble Servant,

COPENHAGEN;   BERNSTORFF.
March the 31st, 1764.

Next to the preceding, the greatest Favour to my Work, in this year, has been granted by His Excellency *The Count De* FIRMIAN Governor of
the

the Milanese, and by *The Marquis* OLIVERA, President of the Senate at Milan; in which city are preserved (in the Ambrosian Library) XII very valuable Hebrew MSS. An excellent Catalogue of these MSS having been taken for me by *Henrico A Porta*, Oriental Professor in the University of *Pavia*; I was very desirous, that these MSS might (if possible) be collated by that learned Gentleman. And he has lately been enabled to enter upon this Work, in consequence of the two following Orders, obligingly passed by the Governor of the Milanese and by the Senate at Milan — that *the Residence of the Professor at Pavia be dispensed with*; and, that *he be allowed to read his Lectures at Milan*: on purpose that he might reside at MILAN, to collate these Ambrosian MSS. The Collation of the first of these MSS has been already sent me; and I am indebted, for the conveyance of it, to the Rev. Dr *Chambers*; to whom it was delivered in Italy by Sir HORATIO MANN. For which, and many other proofs of his Goodness, I am signally obliged to His Excellency; particularly for transmitting also, in this year, the Collations of III MSS, belonging to the Imperial Library, at FLORENCE: where other MSS are now under examination.

As to the Imperial Library, at VIENNA; I have lately been favoured with an account of the Hebrew MSS there, procured of the celebrated Librarian and Physician *Baron Van Swieten*, at the obliging

K   request

requeſt of His Excellency Lord Viſcount Stormont, His Majeſty's Ambaſſador Extraordinary
at that Court. And I have deſired, that a Collation may be undertaken there, particularly of one
MS (containing the whole Bible) which is not de-
ſcribed in the printed Catalogues.

At Rome; out of the XVII MSS ordered to
be there collated, thoſe in the other Libraries (except The Vatican) have been examined; and the
Volume, containing their Various Readings, has
been ſafely conveyed to England, and kindly ſent
me by *Walter Rawlinſon*, Eſq. And as to the parts
of *Daniel* and *Ezra*, printed only in Chaldee, but
which in the Auguſtinian-Angelica MS, now collated, are found alſo in Hebrew; every learned
Reader will hear with pleaſure, that the Hebrew of
theſe large parts (of The Bible) now firſt diſcovered, ſeems very pure, and therefore may be very
antient; and if ſo, muſt be very valuable. Prefixed
to this collection is an ample teſtimony to the care
and accuracy of the Collator, Profeſſor *Conſtanzi*;
ſigned by *Auguſtino Georgi*, *Dominico Theoli*, *Gabriel
Fabricy*, and *Simon Ballerini*: which learned Librarians and Profeſſors will, I hope, accept my Thanks
for their Trouble upon this occaſion. There have
been alſo collated, in this year, VI MSS belonging
to The Vatican.

From the Royal Library at Turin I have now
received the Various Readings of the VI beſt MSS
preſerved

preferved there, which were collated by Profeffor *Pafini* ; for the fafe conveyance of which to England I am obliged to the very learned *The Count De Carburi* : to whofe care they were delivered by *L. Dutens* Efq, the Britifh Refident at that Court.

The Various Readings of the MS at B e r n e, collated under the direction of Mr *Sinner*, the learned Librarian there, have been received. And at Z u r i c h, the Burgo-mafter Regnant Mr *Landolt* has politely granted the Ufe of the II Hebrew MSS, in their public Library; upon an application from *Robert Colebroke* Efq, His Majefty's Refident in *Swifferland* : to whom I am alfo obliged for other marks of his Favour.

In other Foreign Parts (whilft fome of the beft MSS in P a r i s are collating under the care of the celebrated Profeffor L a d v o c a t, at *the Sorbonne* ; and a Collation is alfo making of the Hebrew MS in D r e s d e n) enquiries have been made this year, after other MSS ; and endeavours have been ufed to procure the Ufe of fuch, as are thought the moft valuable. In particular, I muft acknowledge my great Obligations to His Excellency The Earl of R o c h f o r d, His Majefty's Ambaffador Extraordinary to the Court of S p a i n, for his endeavours to procure the Collation of fome MSS in that country. My Thanks are due likewife to my Friend Mr *Devifme*, Chaplain to His Excellency, and alfo to Mr *Pluer*, Chaplain there to the Danifh

Envoy ;

Envoy; who have been very kind in their enquiries after MSS, for the benefit of this Work.

Whilst E u r o p e has thus liberally offered the Treasures of her numerous MSS; and whilst A f r i c a has likewise contributed, in furnishing some MSS before, and now in offering several others, imported through the Munificence and Public-Spirit of H i s D a n i s h M a j e s t y from *Egypt*; it must be observed, that, as enquiries have been making in the *East* upom this same occasion, A s i a also is found to contain what may be of considerable service. For the Lord Bishop of C a r l i s l e having, in the beginning of this year, most obligingly communicated to me a Letter from A l e p p o, containing an account of a very curious MS preserved there; I wrote to the Chaplain to the British Factory, Mr *Dawes* (from whom that Letter to His Lordship came) requesting a more particular information. And I have lately been favoured with his Answer; which represents the MS, as containing the whole Old Testament, and as being of very high Antiquity: and he gives me reason to hope, that an Examination of it there may be granted, in some particular passages; notwithstanding the very extraordinary Veneration paid to it by the Jews. Enquiries have also been made in A m e r i c a : and though hitherto without success, as to MSS of proper Antiquity; yet (I am told) some such Hebrew MSS may possibly be found, amongst the Jews, even in that Quarter of the World.

I cannot conclude this Narrative, without expreffing the fenfe I have of the diftinguifhed Honour done to my Work, by *The Learned Academy*
at MANHEIM; Theirs being the Firft Subfcription, with which this Work has been favoured, in
any Foreign Country.

At Home; the Encouragement given to it has
been SUCH, as requires that the utmoft diligence
and expedition, together with the greateft care and
exactnefs, be continued thro' the remainder of this
Work; which have (I hope) thus far been applied
faithfully: SUCH ENCOURAGEMENT, as demands
from me the warmeft and moft grateful acknowledgments to the PATRONS of the Work, now
living; and the moft honourable expreffions of
duty to the Memory of thofe PATRONS, who
during thefe five years have died — amongft whom
were the following Great PERSONS, from whofe
Patronage this Work has received fignal Advantage
and Honour, and with whofe Illuftrious NAMES
I fhall clofe this Annual Account.

His Grace, The Duke of DEVONSHIRE.

The Right Honourable, The Earls of GRANVILLE,
MACCLESFIELD, BATH, HARDWICKE.

The Right Honourable HENRY BILSON LEGGE.

The Right Reverend, The Bifhops,
HOADLY, SHERLOCK, HAYTER.

The Certificates from Rome *and* Geneva,
originally repeated in this Year's Account,
fee in pages 47, 48.

The Certificate from
The Royal Profeſſor of Hebrew,
nearly the ſame as before,
fee in page 33.

A C C O U N T VI.

At the End of the Year 1765.

THE SIXTH Year, from the beginning of
the Collation of the ſacred Hebrew MSS,
being nearly concluded; I think it my duty, moſt
gratefully to acknowledge the great Encouragement, with which my Work hath thus far been
honourably diſtinguiſhed. And at the ſame time
that I endeavour to expreſs the deep Senſe I have
of my uncommon Obligations, firſt of all to HIS
SACRED MAJESTY, and next to the Illuſtrious
SOCIETIES and Learned PERSONS, who patronize
my Undertaking; I ſhall (as uſual) ſpecify the
Progreſs therein made, for the Satisfaction of Thoſe,
who with ſo much Public-Spirit are pleaſed to
ſubſcribe to it.

After the Experience of one or two Years, in this extensive and laborious Work; it was highly proper that the Patrons of it should be informed, how much time might be necessary for the completion of it. And, after the most careful computation, I acquainted them that the Collation of our own Hebrew MSS, together with some of the best Foreign MSS, to be collated at the same time, would probably be finished in the space of TEN YEARS.

It is with great Pleasure, that I now confirm this computation; and think, that in the next *Four* Years (if but my present State of Health continues) will be collated, not only the rest of the Hebrew MSS before known in Great Britain and Ireland, but also *Five* others — one, in the library of *The Royal Society* — one (a compleat Bible) lately purchased by *Solomon Da Costa Esq*; — two, in *Dublin*; one belonging to *That University*, the other to *the Archiepiscopal library of St Sepulchre*: the knowledge of both which MSS was obligingly communicated to me by Mr Professor Sullivan — and the other is a valuable MS of the whole Bible, written in Syria, and purchased for me at Venice by the Rev. Mr Mordaunt; through whose Care it was safely conveyed to me near twelve months since.

The chief business of the present year has been the Collation of *Seven* MSS, making *Eleven* Volumes;

lumes; which number becomes *Thirteen* by the addition of *Two* Folio Volumes, which are part of another MS. And thefe Seven (omitting the unfinifhed MS) make the whole number of our own MSS hitherto collated F i f t y S e v e n. Of thefe MSS, already collated, Seven contain each the whole Bible; which Seven therefore may contain more Verfes than Twenty other MSS. And it may be added, that the number of Verfes in the MSS, thus far collated, bear a greater proportion to the remainder, than Six years now paft bear to the remaining Four. My Patrons may however be affured, that, without any improper attention to this computation, and without the leaft inclination to protract this Work unneceffarily (for no one perfon in the world can more ardently defire to have it finifhed than I do, partly from long experience of the Fatigue attending it, and partly from a firm conviction of the Utility to be derived from it) the Remainder of the Work fhall be difpatched with the greateft Expedition, confiftent with proper Care: my time being almoft entirely devoted to the difcharge of my duty in the conduct of this Work; to the employment of as many Affiftants as can well be fuperintended at home, and to an extenfive Correfpondence for procuring (at a very large Expence) collations of the beft MSS abroad.

When this Work had been carried on, for fome years; it was found, not only that many of the Variations in the MSS were of confiderable impor-

tance,

tance, but also that the Whole, when collected, would be so very numerous, that there was a necessity for inventing some method singular in its kind, to answer so singular an occasion, as the regular and uncrouded arrangement of all these variations under their respective chapters and verses. In the last year therefore was begun, and in this year has been finished, and is now bound up in 30 Folio Volumes (interleaved) a copy of the printed Hebrew Bible, pasted upon writing paper, with only two verses in each page; the vacant space under each verse being left for all the variations of the MSS in that verse, to be there inserted: and this, according to the numerical order of the MSS, when catalogued and numbered in the Prolegomena to be prefixed to the whole Work. But the Reader is not to infer the number of volumes, which this Work will make hereafter, from the account of this preparatory Bible. For, tho' the Work should at last be comprised in two or three Folio Volumes; and tho' half the Space allowed in this interleaved Bible should prove more than sufficient in general for the variations, together with room for the correction of some mistakes: yet, as some few verses will require the full space here allowed, and it cannot yet be known what those verses may be, it was necessary to prepare a space sufficient for every such exigency.

As to the Transcripts made during the present year, and now deposited in the Bodleian library, in

obedience

obedience to the Order of our Univerſity Delegates; to the number 44, before given in, are now added 17, from the collations of our own MSS. Among the preceding 44 were 4, taken from ſuch Foreign MSS as have been ſent hither to be collated : ſo that, 17 being added to 40, it appears — that *all the Collations of our own MSS*, as yet made, *are now tranſcribed*. For the greater ſafety likewiſe of thoſe Collations, which (for the Benefit of this Work) have been made in various parts of Europe; tranſcripts of theſe alſo, to the number of 17, are now depoſited in the Bodleian library. And the MSS, which have been already collated, and now are under collation for me abroad, amount to between Sixty and Seventy.

Whilſt the collation of the MSS was thus advancing; it was apprehended, that it would be very deſireable, if ſome uſe could likewiſe be made of the beſt Editions already printed. And though it would be evidently impoſſible for me to collate all theſe editions, unleſs in ſelect paſſages; yet it ſeemed neceſſary, that the editions of *Van der Hooght* (here made the Standard) ſhould be collated with that of *Michaelis*, printed at *Hall*, in 1720 : becauſe in this laſt edition, the Variations are already collected from the printed Bibles of *Bomberg, Buxtorf, Stephens,* the *Antwerp* and *London Polyglotts*, and ſeveral other editions : as is ſet forth in *Michaelis Præf.* p. 4 & 5. That the advantage of at leaſt this printed collation might be derived to the preſent Work ; a
collation

collation has been made of the whole text of *Michaelis*, and that of *V. Hooght* : and a tranfcript of this collation is now depofited in the Bodleian library.

The only remaining article, which fhall be here mentioned, as to the State of my Work at home, is this. Every learned Reader muft have been fenfible, that the different Beginnings of feveral Chapters in different Editions have occafioned much trouble in referring to particular Verfes in the Hebrew Bible. And to prevent fuch inconvenience, a collation has alfo been made of the Beginnings of all the Chapters, in the three editions of *V. Hooght*, *Michaelis*, and the *London Polyglott* : and a tranfcript of this collation alfo is now depofited with the others already mentioned.

As to the Collations made, and making, for this Work, during the prefent year, in other Countries; I fhall firft mention the great honour done me by a fecond Letter from his Excellency *The Baron de* B E R N S T O R F F, Principal Secretary of State to His Majefty T H E K I N G O F D E N M A R K. And as the chief Ornament of my laft Account was the Letter fent me by his Excellency ; I fhall give frefh pleafure to all the Patrons of my Work by inferting an exact Copy of this fecond Letter.

Reverend Sir,

  Having received laft September your Letter of Auguft the 14*th, and fome while after, about the end*

       of

of October, the Parcel mentioned therein, containing those Books and Pamphlets You had been so kind as to send hither, and for which I beg You will accept of my sincere Acknowledgments; the Season was then too far advanced, and the short Winter-Days were thought too inconvenient for making, conformably, to your Wishes, Sir, a Beginning with the intended Collation of our Manuscripts. The necessary Measures were taken however, even during that Interval, in order to proceed to the same this Spring, without any further Loss of Time; and it is now that, with the Almighty's Help, the Work is taking in hand. It will be carefully conducted under the Inspection of the Rev. D. D. Holm, Rosenstand-Goiske, and Cramer, Professors of Divinity here, and more particularly under that of Mr Kall, Professor of the Oriental Languages. All the abovesaid MSS have actually been delivered last Week by the King's Orders to these Gentlemen, who, each of them employing several skilful and diligent Subjects, are in hopes to see a great deal of the Collation finished this Year; and when the whole is compleated, You may depend upon its being transmitted to You without the least Delay. I cannot doubt but the Collators will endeavour, by applying themselves to their Task with the utmost Care and Fidelity, to shew themselves worthy of the Trust reposed in them. Meanwhile I have been honoured by your second Letter of February the 14th. Your Annual Accounts of 1763 and 1764 have been duly laid before His Majesty. It affords me a real Pleasure to be able to acquaint You, Rev^d. Sir, with their having met with a very gracious Reception.

Wishing

Wishing You with all my Heart the best of Successes
to your most laudable Undertaking, I am with great
Truth and distinguished Esteem,   Reverend Sir,

Your most obedient humble Servant,

March the 19th, 1764.   B E R N S T O R F F.

At B e r l i n, in the Royal library, a collation
is making of a celebrated MS in 4 Folio Volumes;
part of which collation I have received from Profeffor *Murfinna*. In the fame Royal library is preferved an Hebrew Bible, in 8vo *printed*; an edition, older by above 20 years than any printed
Hebrew Bible known here in *England.* This, which
was the Copy from whence the famous Luther
made his Verfion, contains feveral hundred Variations from the Hebrew Bibles, fince printed; and
I have therefore defired a compleat collation of it
to be made by Profeffor *Schulze*, to whom I am
much obliged for an account of this curious Book:
and the world will be foon favoured with a Differtation upon it by this learned Profeffor. But for
the advantages at Berlin, I am particularly indebted
to the very reverend Mr *Sack*, firft Chaplain to His
Majefty T h e K i n g o f P r u s s i a : and this
zealous Friend, who has furnifhed me with many
ufeful notices, has been alfo at confiderable Expence, which he generoufly prefents to my Work
as *His Subfcription.*

At

At ERFURT are some Hebrew MSS, which were collated for the edition of *Michaelis* before-mentioned; and concerning *their* Various Readings, the following Remarks seem necessary. Having often observed with surprize, that the Variations, which in this Bible are published from these Erfurt MSS, are very trifling as well as few, in comparison of those in most other Hebrew MSS; I strongly suspected, that the Erfurt Variations were not properly represented in the Notes to that printed Bible, but that many Variations, particularly those of greater Moment, were omitted. My Friend, the justly celebrated Professor *Michaelis*, of Gottingen, hearing of my suspicion, and being told that I had fixed upon two instances, found upon examination that these MSS contained many Variations not printed, and in particular the very Readings I had specified: in testimony of which he most obligingly sent me two Certificates signed and sealed at Erfurt. I have therefore requested, that these MSS may be more fairly and fully represented to the Public, by an entire re-collation of them at my expence. And I doubt not, but such *future* collation will be as serviceable to my Work, as the *last* might have been urged to the discredit of collating Hebrew MSS in general.

In the Imperial library at VIENNA is a compleat MS of the Bible, not mentioned in any printed Catalogue; which has been collated for me by the learned *Aloysius de Sonnenfels:* and the Collation has been moft carefully fent me by His Excellency Lord Vifcount STORMONT, His Majefty's Ambaffador Extraordinary at that Court.

At COLOGNE there is alfo a MS of the whole Bible, which is now collating at my requeft : and for this permiffion I am highly obliged to the Rev. Dr *Hillefheim*, Rector of the College, who has favoured me with an account of this MS, and a *Fac Simile* of its character.

At FLORENCE has been lately finifhed, by the learned Fathers *Berretta* and *Bartoli*, a compleat MS of the Bible ; the Collation of which has been very obligingly brought to England, at the Requeft of His Excellency Sir HORATIO MANN, by the Rev. Mr *Hamilton :* who alfo brought the Various Readings of the fecond and third Hebrew MSS, collated by the learned Profeffor *A Porta*, in the *Ambrofian* Library at MILAN.

At ROME, the learned *Conftanzi* has now executed my fecond commiffion there ; which was for collating 17 MSS, 12 of which are preferved in the Vatican. For the Ufe of the MSS in this celebrated Library, I gratefully acknowledge myfelf indebted to the Goodnefs and Patronage of His Eminence Cardinal ALBANI. And, as all my Patrons will be pleafed with knowing, that the prefent Protector of the Vatican fucceeded Cardinal PASSIONEI, not only in Office, but alfo in Zeal for my Work ; I fhall acquaint them with my Obligations.

ligations. In the first Letter, with which His Eminence honoured me, He was pleased to say — *Et
vojant jusqu'ou vous avez en si peu de tems avancé
un Ouvrage si fraieux et penible, je ne puis si non
vous feliciter de tout mon cœur de l' heureux succès d'
une entreprise, qui rendra votre nom immortel à la pos-
terité plus reculée, et dont la Republique des Lettres
tirera tant de profit et de lumieres.* And some time
after, in answer to my application for a *second* Collation in the Vatican, His Eminence (then *Cardinal-
Librarian*) condescended to write the following
Letter; which I here insert, instead of that hitherto
inserted from Cardinal PASSIONEI.

*Quas ad me dedisti humanissimas Literas calendis
Decembris, accepi Vir clar. et quam moleste ab iis in-
tellexi te gravi correptum morbo in discrimine fuisse,
tantundem ex animo gratulor te plene convaluisse. Me-
dicorum autem, quorum operâ ereptus es, consilium am-
plectaris velim, temperando nimirum a literariis laboribus, ne nimius in illis ardor valetudini tuæ officiat;
quantum enim literariæ Reipublicæ ut insigne Opus
tuum vulgetur, tantundem mea interest ut diu vivas
incolumis. Jus erit Professori Constantio tot codicum
collationem instituere, quot Vaticana Bibliotheca com-
plectitur; illique tradam codicum indicem, quem misisti,
ut illos quantocius scrutetur. Quod me jussis honestes
tuis, idque equidem ut crebro facias, oro: Deumque
O. M. enixe rogo, Te ad seros annos servet incolumem.*

Romæ,
Cal. Febr. 1763. ALEXANDER *Card.* ALBANUS.

What has been lately done at PARIS, I have not yet been informed particularly; on account of the Death of that eminent Promoter of this Work and my zealous Friend, the learned and worthy Librarian of the *Sorbonne*, Profeſſor LADVOCAT. But, notwithſtanding this affecting Loſs; I cannot doubt of conſiderable Aſſiſtance from that City. For, being very deſirous, that ſome of the beſt MSS in the Royal Library there might be collated for my Work, I this year applied to His Excellency *The Earl of* HERTFORD, His Majeſty's late Ambaſſador Extraordinary at the Court of *France*; who immediately obtained Leave, and in the moſt obliging manner honoured me with the notice of it, and with the Letter of *The Count de St* FLORENTIN. My grateful Thanks are alſo due to His Excellency *The Duke de* NIVERNOIS; who applied likewiſe for the Royal MSS, and preſented to HIS MAJESTY the laſt Annual Account of my Work. The ſecond Letter, which his Excellency condeſcended to write to me, will acquaint my Patrons with the Honour thus done me by this Ornament and Patron of Literature *The Duke de* NIVERNOIS, and the gracious acceptance of my Annual Account by ſo great a Monarch as HIS SOVEREIGN.

A Paris, le 3 *Mar.* 1765.
Je n'ay pas manqué de remettre adjourd'huy au Roy, Monſieur, un Exemplaire du compte que vous avés rendu cette année des progrès de votre ouvrage. S. Majeſté a
M   *reçu*

*reçu ce preſent avec plaiſir, et m'a chargé de vous le
temoigner. J'ay remis auſſi a M. de S. Florentin l'exemplaire que vous m'avés adreſé pour luy. Ce Miniſtre
concourera bien volontiers a tout ce qui pourra accelerer
la confe&tion d'un ſi important ouvrage. Je ſouhaite,
Monſieur, avoir reuſſi par mon Zele a executer vos
ordres a vous donner une nouvelle preuve de mon dévoüe-
ment ſincere, et de tous les ſentiments avec les quels
j'ay l'honneur d'etre tres parfaitement, Monſieur,
votre tres humble et tres obeiſſant Serviteur,*

LE DUC DE NIVERNOIS.

The laſt State of my Work mentioned my particular Obligation to *The Learned Academy* at MAN-
HEIM; and I now gratefully acknowledge the
Favour of THE ELECTOR PALATINE: for, at
the Recommendation of His Serene Highneſs, I
have lately obtained an account of an Hebrew MS
at *Mentz*, which was drawn up by the learned Mr
Goldhagen. This account has been ſent me by my
friend Mr *D'Harold*, at the Court of Manheim;
to whom I am alſo indebted for a very obliging
Letter from Mr *Schmidtz*, Counſellor to the MAR-
GRAVE of *Baden-Durlac*, relative to two curious
MSS in His Highneſs's Library.

Laſtly: in the enumeration of Services and Enquiries for the Benefit of this Work, during the
preſent year; very grateful mention muſt be made
of the Favour of His Excellency, The Honourable
Sir JOSEPH YORKE, His Majeſty's Ambaſſador

Extra-

Extraordinary at the Hague, in relation to fome
valuable MSS at *Utrecht*.

In confequence of fuch numerous and fingular
Obligations, it is certainly my duty to exert my
utmoft endeavours for the perfection of my Work,
and the fatisfaction of all the Patrons of it : and
as fome of them have, in the laft year, mentioned
to me two circumftances, I will take notice of both
in this place. It has been faid — that it would be
agreeable to the prefent, and might procure more,
Subfcribers ; if fome *Specimen* were to be printed,
now and then, to prove the Importance of the Work
by the Various Readings collected from the MSS.
But I muft obferve, that a regular Specimen of any
part of the Bible is at prefent impoffible ; becaufe
Acceffions are making to every part continually.
And let be obferved farther, that I have already
communicated to the Public, at different times,
above 300 inftances of fuch Various Readings ;
many of which are fo important, that thofe Perfons,
who cannot be convinced by *them*, will certainly
not be convinced by 300 more. And as to thofe,
who were at all convinced, that this Work was
proper to be *undertaken* ; fuch, it is prefumed,
muft ftill think it worth *finifhing* and *publifhing*.

The other circumftance, mentioned in this year,
is — that, a particular account of the Expence not
being annually printed, it has been infinuated, that
this Work is perhaps carried on with *very little* or

no

no Expence; at leaft, not with an Expence at all proportioned to the Subfcription. To this I fay, firft, that I do by no means defire any one Perfon to entruft me with his Money, who doubts my proper Application of it. And I beg leave to add, for the perfect Satisfaction of all my Subfcribers, that (exclufive of the Collations of many other MSS already engaged for in different Parts of Europe) my Expences, in this one Year, on account of this Work, amount to above Six Hundred Pounds; the greater part of which is ftanding and conftant Expence, in every Year.

I fhall now conclude this Annual Account with part of an Elogium upon my *Work* and it's Patrons, delivered in a Public Oration, at *Hall* in *Saxony,* by the reverend and learned Dr Semler, Profeffor of Divinity in that Univerfity.

Cum ampliffima illa exornandi Hebraici codicis provincia, quam Celeb. Kennicotum apud Anglos, primum rite, melioribus certe aufpiciis quam ante ipfum quenquam, fufcepiffe fcimus, non folum eorum omnium excipiatur publicis plaufibus, qui in Romana Ecclefia liberali eruditioni non obfcure favere videntur, fed etiam deditiffimis ftudiis ultro promoveatur: dubitari non poteft, nec inter nos defuturos, qui tantæ et tam præclaræ rei fucceffus profperos, votis ominibufque lætis, publice privatimque adjutum eant. —Jam vel inter eos, quibus litterarum facrarum difciplina traditur, gratulari fibi folet, quotus quifque eft erectioris ingenii; quod hæc vi-
                                                                    vendo

vendo tempora attigerit, quibus Publicum quaſi Signum erectum eſt, ad bene ſperandum de amplificanda Hebraici codicis dignitate. — Equidem varie affici ſoleo, cum luculentiſſima illa ſtudia cogito, quæ in Anglia, beata pluribus nominibus Inſula, publice privatimque ingenti contentione ad hanc cauſam promovendam conferuntur. R E G I S illius Auguſtiſſimi ſplendidiſſimam munificentiam facile nobis fingimus : ſcimus enim Angliæ Regem eſſe. A C A D E M I A R U M Britanniæ utriuſque illuſtrem ac venuſtum conſenſum, in adjuvando Kennicoti propoſito, quis non admiretur? T R E S Academiæ omnes lubentiſſime votis ejus occurrunt. Ibi Reverendiſſimi A R C H I E P I S C O P I liberaliſſime condicunt ſumtus. Nobiliſſimi P R I N C I P E S, Honoratiſſimi C O-M I T E S, ultro conferunt. Reverendorum E P I S C O P O-R U M et D E C A N O R U M exiſtit fauſta concordia. B A R O N E S, A R M I G E R I, privati adeo Religionis A D M I N I S T R I, numero longo in Societatem hanc coeunt.

Fortunatos, felices ibi eruditos !

The C E R T I F I C A T E

from

The Royal Profeſſor of Hebrew,

nearly the ſame as before,

ſee in page 33.

ACCOUNT VII.

At the End of the Year 1766.

INTRODUCTION,
nearly the same as before,
see in page 78.

TO the number of FIFTY SEVEN MSS,
collated in the Six Years preceding, are to
be now added, as having been collated in the present Year, THIRTEEN; so that the whole number of MSS at home, now collated, amounts to
SEVENTY. And, as to those MSS at home,
which remain unexamined; I hope, and believe,
they will be all collated during *the Three next Years.*

Of the Thirteen MSS, examined during this
Year, *Six* belong to *The British Museum*; lent me
in consequence of an Order at a General Meeting
of The Curators of that invaluable Repository,
where only *Four* now remain to be collated: *One*
MS has been lent me by the Dean and Chapter of
Wells: and *One* Copy, which, tho' printed, is really
more valuable than several of our present MSS,
has been this Year lent by the Provost and Fellows
of *Eton* College, out of their elegant and valuable
Library.

Library. And for the Use of all these Books, communicated in the most obliging manner, I publickly express my Thanks.

But amongst all the Obligations of this nature, conferred during the present Year, there is One, which demands my particular and most grateful Acknowledgments. And these I here make, in the most dutiful and most humble manner, to HIS MAJESTY, for the Use of a very antient and curious *printed* Hebrew Pentateuch; which HIS MAJESTY has most graciously commanded to be lent me from His Royal Library. The Collation of this Pentateuch is begun; and this Edition, together with a few others likewise very antient, will be particularly described near the conclusion of this Account.

The last annual Account mentioned, that *Transcripts* of the Collations of *Fifty Seven* of our own MSS were then deposited in the Bodleian Library; together with those of *Four* foreign MSS collated here, and of *Seventeen* collated in other parts of Europe. To the preceding Fifty Seven are now added *Eleven*, and to the Twenty One are added *Nineteen*; so that the whole number of Transcripts, which I have now deposited in the Bodleian Library, amounts to ONE HUNDRED AND EIGHT.

The MSS at home and abroad, now collated for this Work, amount to ONE HUNDRED AND THIRTY;

THIRTY; and even thefe, it is prefumed, are more
than ever were made ufe of, to afcertain the true
Text of any other book in the world. But yet,
that this Work may as far exceed all others in the
Quantity of its Materials, as it does in the Great-
nefs of that Patronage by which it is fupported;
not only the remaining MSS will be finifhed at
home, but alfo many other valuable MSS will be
collated in other countries: and as to thefe, the
Collation of between *Twenty* and *Thirty* is at prefent engaged for.

An examination of the MSS, very fortunately
procured from the Eaft, at the Command of His
Majefty The late K I N G O F D E N M A R K, is now
making at C O P E N H A G E N by fome learned Profeffors, who were appointed by His Excellency
The Baron de B E R N S T O R F F, an Illuftrious Patron
of this Work. The celebrated *Abbé Hooke*, who
fucceeds the late Profeffor *Ladvocat* in Zeal for this
Work, as well as in the Hebrew Chair at the Sorbonne, has informed me that the two MSS, which
I have felected as being probably the moft valuable
at P A R I S, one in the *Royal* library, and the other
at the *Oratory*, are both under examination; in confequence of an order from H I S M O S T C H R I S T I A N
M A J E S T Y as to the former; and by the favour of
the learned Fathers of the Oratory, as to the latter.
A collation of the MS at C A S S E L, diftinguifhed
by Mr Scheide's Differtation upon it, is in part
made; and that part has been received from *Goet-*
tingen:

tingen: for, upon leave given by His Serene Highnefs The L A N D G R A V E of H E S S E, that MS has
been removed by my very learned Friend Profeffor
Michaelis, who kindly took a journey to Caffel, for
the more fecure conveyance of it to Goettingen.
And (not to enlarge, by fpecifying more at prefent) the two famous MSS, formerly belonging to
Reuchlin, now in the library of the M A R G R A V E
of B A D E N - D U R L A C, at the Palace of *Carlfruhe,*
have been this year committed to the care of Mr
Bruns, by the Honourable Mr *Schmidtz* Privy-
Counfellor to His Serene Highnefs.

I muft here exprefs my acknowledgments to
Monf. L'Abbé le Blond, for his great care in tranfcribing and fending me from *Caen* the collations of
S I X MSS of the Pfalms, examined at P A R I S under
the direction of the late Profeffor *Ladvocat.* The
celebrated Profeffor *Breitinger,* at Z U R I C H, has
alfo been very obliging by his zeal and fervice ;
not only in freely collating for me great part of a
MS at *Zurich,* but alfo in procuring me the Various Readings of a MS (not before known to the
Public) preferved in *the Monaftery of St Blafe* in
the Black Foreft ; the collation of which was very
politely ordered by the illuftrious Prince and Prelate M A R T I N I, who is therefore entitled to my
gratitude : the fame is due likewife to *William
Norton Efq;* His Majefty's Minifter to the Swifs
Cantons, for fending me both thefe collations. And
I muft alfo exprefs my thanks to *Sir Horace Mann,*

N   *Bart.*

Bart. His Majefty's Refident at Florence, for tranf-
mitting the collations of fome MSS finifhed at
M I L A N, by Profeffor *A Porta* and Dr *Baptifta
Branca*; which collations were brought me, in a
very obliging manner, by the Honourable *Sir
William Stanhope.*

In return for the very generous Subfcription, by
which this Work has been eminently diftinguifhed;
one part of my duty certainly is, to acquaint the
P A T R O N S of it with any fignal marks of Approbation fhewn to it by the Learned World. And I
fhall therefore, for the Satisfaction of my S U B-
S C R I B E R S, infert copies of two Inftruments I have
lately been favoured with; and which I have been
favoured with on account of that Work, in which,
through T H E I R Encouragement, I have the Honour to be employed.

In the prefent year a Difcovery has been made,
which is of great importance in itfelf, and moft
nearly connected with the nature of this Work;
and as it unfolds a new, yet decifive argument, in
proof of the *Expediency,* or rather the *Neceffity* of
fuch an Undertaking, particular notice muft be
here taken of it: and it may be rendered more
generally intelligible, in confequence of the following introduction.

The Learned thro' Europe have been long di-
vided into two general claffes, as to their opinions
of *the printed Hebrew Text of the Old Teftament*;

fome

some infisting upon the absolute Integrity of that Text, others holding it to be in some instances corrupted. The men of this latter class were subdivided in their sentiments; for while some thought the corruptions few and of little moment, others thought them many and of great consequence. In this however they almost all agreed, that, whatever was the real number, or nature, of the corruptions in the printed Text, *that Text could receive little or no correction from Hebrew MSS*; because the Hebrew MSS, now extant, were but few; and these few were modern; and all of them entirely, or nearly, the same with one another and with the Text as printed. But this opinion, however prevalent till within a few years past, has been so effectually confuted by the evidence produced from these MSS, that the common opinion (it is presumed) now is — that the Hebrew MSS, yet extant, are *very many*; and that some *differ greatly* from others, and from the printed Text.

Now amongst all these variations of opinion, it has been taken for granted by all parties, that *the Text of the Hebrew Bible, as now* PRINTED, *is one and uniform; entirely, or nearly, the same in all the editions of it*; wherever, and by whomsoever, it has hitherto been published. And upon this imaginary Sameness of all the printed copies has been founded the famous notion, formerly asserted by many, and even now by a few, that *the printed Hebrew Text is perfect and uncorrupted*. Whereas,

N 2

on the contrary; if that very Text, as it is now printed, be at laſt found to vary much from itſelf, and ſome copies differ greatly from others; then can there be nothing more abſurd, than the notion of all the printed copies being pure and genuine: then can nothing be more clear, than that, whenever one printed copy differs from another, this or that copy muſt be corrupted: and laſtly, nothing can be more certain, than that, in caſe theſe differences be many and conſiderable, *it muſt be our duty to examine* (or cauſe to be examined) *as many as poſſible of the oldeſt and beſt MSS*; in order to determine, with a degree of exactneſs proportioned to the Importance of the Subject, which of the printed editions are wrong, and which right, where they are found to differ. And, in order to ſuch determination, the beſt method (which indeed is propoſed to be here taken) ſeems to be — to republiſh the Hebrew Text, exactly as it now ſtands in one of the beſt amongſt the common Editions; and to ſubjoin at the bottom of each page (ſo far as relates to each page) all the Various Readings, which ſhall have been collected either from the MSS, or the printed Copies.

The many and conſiderable Differences here meant, as found in *the printed Copies* themſelves, are (not typographical errors, or variations amongſt the ſeveral modern editions, but) ſuch as remarkably diſtinguiſh the modern Copies from the moſt antient. It had been before diſcovered, in the

courſe

courfe of this Work, that the older the MSS are, the more they differ from the modern printed Text, and the more they agree with the Antient Verfions and the Quotations in the New Teftament. And it is now found, that *the oldeft printed* copies differ greatly from *the lateft* ; and agree moft with *the oldeft and beft* MSS. It is to the enquiries of the prefent Year, that the Learned are indebted for this difcovery, as to the Merit and Value of the OLDEST PRINTED copies ; and the proof arifes from the joint authorities of the Four following Editions.

The *firft* is the E T O N copy, mentioned before as collated in the prefent year ; and indeed it has, for greater exactnefs, been collated twice. It was printed as early as 1487, and is probably the only copy in the world of this edition ; the Various Readings in this from Vander Hooght's edition are very numerous, and feveral of real confequence. But, as a fingle evidence in fuch a caufe would not be fufficiently fatisfactory, the *fecond* old edition, which I fhall mention, was printed in 1494 ; and that copy of it, which belonged to L U T H E R, is now in the Royal Library at B E R L I N : and at my requeft a collation of it is nearly finifhed by the celebrated Profeffor *Schulze*, who has publifhed a curious Volume concerning it, in the German language ; to which is prefixed an Englifh Dedication, for which I publickly exprefs my thanks. The German Volume has been moft obligingly tranflated

for

for me, into Latin, by the reverend and learned
Mr *Woide* ; and by the help of this verfion I find,
that this *Berlin* Bible differs exceedingly from the
modern copies : near 500 variations in whole *Words*
or *Letters* being fpecified in this Differtation, and
above 200 inftances of difference in the Maforetical
Points. Many of the verbal and literal differences
agree with the readings of the *Eton* copy ; and feveral are of confiderable moment. The *third* and
fourth copies, which I fhall mention, are the FIRST
*edition that ever was printed of the whole Hebrew
Bible*, being printed in 1488 ; and a Pentateuch,
in 1492 : which books are happily preferved in the
library of His Serene Highnefs The MARGRAVE
of BADEN-DURLAC. This very acceptable intelligence I have lately received from Mr *Bruns* before-
mentioned, together with fpecimens of the Variations of thefe two Editions : and I find, that thefe
Editions concur with the two former, in differing
greatly from the modern Editions, and are more
agreeable to the oldeft and beft MSS. Thefe two
copies alfo will be collated, for the greater perfection of this Work ; and from thefe, with the two
former, will be collected a multitude of material
Various Readings. And it is obfervable ; that,
though thefe four copies fo much agree, yet they
ftill vary enough to fhew, that they were not printed from one another, but from different MSS.

I fhall clofe this article with earneftly requefting
the Learned, in foreign countries as well as in our
own,

own, that they will favour me with any fuch notices as are yet wanting, in order to a more compleat
difcovery of the State of the Oldeft Editions. And,
as I fhall be greatly obliged to Them for acquainting me, either with fuch of thofe Editions as I have
not heard of, or with the Places where any of thofe
Editions are preferved of which I do not at prefent
know the Places; I fhall lay before Them the following Table — not of *all* the Editions of either
the Whole or Parts of the Hebrew Bible, which
preceded the firft Maforetical Bible in 1528 (all
which amount to near FIFTY) but of fuch only,
as were printed before the famous Editions of *Cardinal Ximenes* at *Complutum* in 1517, and of *Felix
Pratenfis* at *Venice* in 1518.

1486 — PROPHETS — in folio, printed at *Soncino*,
    no points; did belong to the late famous
    Rabbi *Oppenheim*, at *Hanover*: but the place,
    where it is now preferved, is not known to me.

1487 — HAGIOGRAPHA — 2 Vol. folio, at *Naples*,
    on Vellum, pointed almoft throughout; pre-
    ferved in *Eton* College library.

1488 — BIBLE — folio, at *Soncino*, with points;
    in the library of His Serene Highnefs the
    Margrave of *Baden-Durlac*.

— BIBLE — dated this year, catalogued as
printed at *Bologna*, is faid to be preferved in
the *Barberini* library at *Rome*.

— BIBLE

— BIBLE — dated this year, is faid to be preferved in the IMPERIAL *Laurentian* library at *Florence*.

1491 — PENTATEUCH — 2 Vol. folio, at *Lifbon*, on Vellum, pointed; having the Chaldee Paraphrafe and Jarchi's Commentary: belongs to the library of His Majefty THE KING OF GREAT BRITAIN.

— PENTATEUCH — folio, with the Chaldee Paraphrafe and Jarchi's Commentary, belongs to the Royal library at *Paris*; and, tho' catalogued as printed in 1490 (which perhaps is the date at the end of the *firft* volume) feems another copy of the edition of 1491: which is the date at the end of the *fecond* volume. And in His MOST CHRISTIAN MAJESTY'S library is preferved another copy; the defcription of which more exactly agrees with that of the preceding edition, belonging to HIS BRITANNIC MAJESTY.

1492 — PENTATEUCH, MEGILLOTH & HAPH. — 8°, at *Brefcia*; in the library of The Margrave of *Baden-Durlac*.

1493 — PRIOR PROPHETS — folio, at *Naples*; place, where now preferved, unknown.

1494 — BIBLE — 8°, at *Brefcia*; in the library of His Majefty THE KING OF PRUSSIA.

— BIBLE — dated this year, reprefented as printed at *Pefaro*, unpointed, is faid to be in the *Caroline* library at *Zurich*.

— Kings — folio, at *Leiria*; in the Royal
library at *Paris*.

1497 — Isaiah & Jeremiah — folio, at *Lisbon*;
place, where now preserved, unknown.

— Proverbs — folio; did belong to *Oppenheim*: place, where now preserved, unknown.

1511 — Prior Prophets — (and *Posterior*,
according to *Le Long*) — folio, at *Pesaro*; in
the Royal library at *Paris*.

1513 — Isaiah & Jeremiah — folio, at *Constantinople*; place, where now preserved, unknown.

1515 — Pentateuch & Megilloth — place,
where now preserved, unknown.

— Psalms, Proverbs, Job, & Daniel —
folio, at *Thessalonica*; preserved in The *Bodleian*.

1516 — Posterior Prophets — folio, 2ᵈ edit.
at *Pesaro*; in the library of the Reverend
Mr *Sanford*.

— Psalms — folio, at *Genoa*; one of FIFTY
different printed editions of the Whole or
Parts of the Hebrew Bible, which have been
purchased by myself.

— Psalms — folio, at *Basil*; in vol. 8 of
St *Jerom*'s Works.

— Psalms — 18°, at *Basil*; in the library
at *Dantzic*.

O   — Job

— J o b — 4°, at *Paris*; place, where preferved, unknown.

1517 — B i b l e — folio, 2 columns, by one of
the *Soncinates* ; did belong to *Oppenheim* :
place, where now preferved, unknown.

Then follow, as finished in 1517 and 1518, the
Two Editions of
The Complutensian Polyglott Bible
And The
Venice (Bomberg) Bible by Felix Pratensis.

NOTE. The Date, in the oldeft editions, is
generally at the End of the volumes, and inferted
after the word רבש *year of*; and, tho' it be fometimes given in words at length, is oftner expreffed
in the numeral letters of the Hebrew Alphabet.
The Jews reckon, from the Creation, 240 years
lefs than are ufually reckoned by Chriftians : and
therefore, if a book be dated *from the Creation*
5246 ; by deducting 3760, the fum left is the year
of Chrift 1486, which is the time of the firft printed
edition. But if, as is generally the cafe, the Printer
gives *the leffer computation* by leaving out the thoufands, and expreffes only 246; then by adding 1000,
with 240 the difference of reckoning, the year of
Chrift is found 1486, as before. Thus : the Date
of the oldeft edition being 1486, a copy of it will
probably be known by the letters רמו *i.e.* 246, or
by other letters making the fame number: a copy,
printed in 1494, may be known by רנד 254, or
other numerals of the fame amount: one, in 1500,
by רס 260 : and one, in 1517, by רעז 277.

DIPLOMA from GOETTINGEN.

Quod immortaliter promeritus eſt de critica textus Hebraici Benjamin Kennicott, *Theologiæ Doctor in Univerſitate Oxonienſi, Societatis Regiæ Britannicæ Socius, Sociuſque Collegii Exonienſis ; conquiſitis per omnem Europam, quin immo ex Africæ Aſiæque oris, codicibus librorum priſci fœderis, nondum in hunc finem adhibitis, iiſdemque vel ipſo proſpiciente domi, vel blando ejus impulſu apud exteros, diligentiſſime collatis: eas ob res* SOCIETAS REGIA SCIENTIARUM GOETTINGENSIS Benjaminum Kennicott, *Theologiæ Doctorem in Univerſitate Oxonienſi,* COLLEGIS CLASSIS PHILOLOGICÆ *adſcripſit, adſcriptum hoc documento declarat; petens ab eo, ut criticos in codicem Hebraicum labores, feliciſſimo auſu ſuſceptos, pari ſtudio ad finem perducat, editionemque aliquando exhibeat illis copiis inſtructam, quibus nullus unquam liber inſtructus prodiit. Ex quo ſucceſſu permagnam certe lætitiam ſentiet, eundemque Sodali impenſe gratulabitur Societas; ipſius viciſſim erga ſe voluntatem urgens, et demonſtratam officiis mutuis compenſatura.* GOETTINGÆ; 27 *Januar.* 1766.

Sigill.

JOANNES DAVID MICHAELIS, *Societatis Regiæ Director.*

S.R.S. Goett.

JOAN. PHIL. MURRAY, *Phil. Prof. Ord. Societatiſq; Reg. Scientiar. Secretarius.*

DIPLOMA from MANNHEIM.

Academiæ ELECTORALIS *Scientiarum & Elegant.*
Literarum THEODORO-PALATINÆ *Præses,*
Director ac Socii, Lecturis S.

*Cum eadem omnium sit Veritas, eòque in rerum na-
tura nihil præstantius; commune esse debet Veritatis
studium, et communis investigationis honos. Centrum
quasi hujus tum studii, tum honoris, recte habentur So-
cietates literariæ, a Principibus viris solenni quodam
modo constitutæ, membrisque compositæ variis, quorum
alia tegendis et promovendis laboribus Academicis, alia
propius iis subeundis, alia remotius, sunt destinata.
Legibus hinc nostris tres Sociorum ordinatæ sunt Classes;
quæ, quo inter se erunt conjunctiores, eo facilius me-
tam Veritatis propositam attingent. Prima classis est
Ordinariorum, quindecim numero, Societatis anima;
cui ornamento accedit secunda Honorariorum, et auxilio
classis Extraordinariorum tertia. Inter Extraordina-
rios hos, annuente* SERENISSIMO CAROLO THEO-
DORO, *Principe Electore, cooptatus a nobis est Vir
antiquarum literarum doctissimus,* Benjaminus Kennicott, S. T. P. *Regiæque Societatis Anglicanæ ut et
Collegii Exoniensis Socius percelebris, Academiæ nostræ
ab incunabulis inde suis amicissimus: unde hoc Socii
Extraordinarii Diploma, Sigillo Academico nostro mu-
nitum, scribi et tradi ei lubentissime curavimus. Dat.*
MANNHEMII; VI *Cal. Maii,* 1766.

LEOPOLDUS L.B.   *Sigill.*   STENGEL.
DE HOHENHAUSEN.   *Acad. Mann.*   LAMEY.

The CERTIFICATE:

Which is here given, as containing the Second
Renewal of our Univerſity Subſcription.

THE Delegates of the Preſs, in the Univerſity of
Oxford, having in January 1760 ſubſcribed to Dr
Kennicott's Collation of the Hebrew MSS ; and having
inſerted in an Order then made the following words [*That
their Subſcription be continued at the beginning of every Year,
upon Dr Kennicott's producing a Certificate from the Royal
Profeſſor of Hebrew, that in his Judgment Dr Kennicott hath
made a competent Progreſs in the ſaid Work during the Year
preceding* ;] and the ſaid Delegates, as well as the Uni-
veſity of Cambridge, having in the beginning of the preſent
Year again renewed their Subſcription to this Work on
condition of a Certificate from me, as before-mentioned ;
and Dr Kennicott having applied to me for ſuch a Certificate : I do hereby accordingly Certify, for the Satisfaction of both theſe Univerſities, and of ſuch Perſons as
have encouraged this Work by their Subſcriptions, that
the ſeveral Parts of the Collation, made during this Seventh
Year, have been laid before me ; and my Opinion is,
that Dr Kennicott hath made a very competent Progreſs
in the ſaid Collation. And, upon conſidering ſeveral of the
Various Readings, which he has already diſcovered in the
Hebrew MSS ; I think this Work will be of very conſiderable Service to Sacred Literature.

THO. HUNT,

Chriſt-Church ;
Decemb. 30, 1766.

Regius Profeſſor of Hebrew.

Account VIII.

At the End of the Year 1767.

IT is with great pleasure, that I now wait upon the Illustrious and Learned PATRONS of my Collation of the Hebrew MSS of the Old Testament; in order to lay before Them the *Progress* made in the Work, and the *Encouragement* with which it has been honoured, in the present year, which is the EIGHTH from the beginning of this Undertaking.

To the number of Seventy MSS, collated in the 7 years preceding, are to be now added FIFTEEN; so that the whole number of MSS at home, now collated, amounts to EIGHTY FIVE. And as to the MSS at home, yet unexamined; I hope, and believe, they will be all collated during the two next years. And, if so; then will this Collation have been singularly fortunate : as being compleated in the very time, which, upon a Calculation at first made, I declared to be necessary, namely TEN YEARS.

Of the 15 MSS, now collated, *Four* belong to *The British Museum*, and are the whole (out of the

the 28 in that invaluable Repoſitory) which re-
mained uncollated : *Three* other MSS belong to
the Library of *The Royal Society* ; and *Six* to the
Library of *Corpus Chriſti College*, in Oxford. And
for the uſe of all theſe MSS, communicated in the
moſt obliging manner, I publickly expreſs my
thanks. I muſt here alſo make my acknowledgments to The Maſter and Fellows of *St John's
College*, in Cambridge ; who have lately lent me
Two valuable MSS : which, not being yet collated, are not included in the number before ſpecified.

During the laſt year it was happily diſcovered,
that the *printed* Hebrew Bibles differed greatly
from each other ; and that the *moſt early* editions
had many and important Variations, agreeably to
the *more antient* MSS ; whilſt the *modern* editions
agree only with the *lateſt* MSS. The oldeſt editions
therefore being very valuable, and abſolutely neceſſary to be collated likewiſe ; I beg leave to expreſs my gratitude in the moſt dutiful manner, to
HIS MAJESTY, The Royal and Munificent
Patron of this Work, for the Uſe of an antient
and very curious *Pentateuch*, upon fine vellum, one
of the moſt elegant Books that ever came from
the Preſs (for there are proofs of its being *printed*,
tho' it has frequently been taken for *a MS*) which
HIS MAJESTY graciouſly commanded to be
lent me at the end of the laſt year, and which was
collated in the beginning of the preſent.

Three

Three years before this Royal Pentateuch, which is dated in 1491, there was printed the *first* edition of *the whole Hebrew Bible* ; and of this Bible only 3 copies were known in Europe, till a fourth was fortunately purchafed, this year, by my very learned Friend *Mr* SANFORD, of *Balliol* College. The Collation of this printed Bible is already fo far advanced as to fhew, that it is exceedingly valuable; and it certainly contains fome thoufands of Variations, feveral of which are of confiderable confequence : a decifive confutation this of the opinion, which, till within a year or two paft, obtained univerfally among the Learned, that *all the printed Hebrew Bibles were entirely or nearly the fame*. On this very interefting article of the oldeft printed editions, I fhall obferve farther, that to the catalogue of them given in my laft Account are to be now added, not only this firft whole Bible dated in 1488, but alfo another copy of the ETON *Hagiographa*, of 1487, preferved in the *Cafanatenfian* library at *Rome* ; and alfo 2 others (both older than that of the *Prophets* in 1486) — one, containing *Jofh. Judg. & Sam.* in 1484, which I have myfelf feen in The *Royal* Library at *Paris* — and the other a *Pentateuch*, in 1482, which *Maffei* fays (*Veron. Illuftrat.* 3, 7) is preferved at *Verona* : and there is another copy of this Pentateuch in the curious Library of His Serene Highnefs *The Margrave of* BADEN-DURLAC, at the palace of *Carlf-ruhe*.

rabe. * Hence then it appears, that the method, which feems to have been originally obferved in printing the Hebrew Bible, was juft what might have been expected; firft, the *Pentateuch*, in 1482; fecondly, the *Prior Prophets*, in 1484; thirdly, the *Pofterior Prophets*, in 1486; and fourthly, the *Hagiographa*, in 1487: and, after the 4 great parts had been thus printed feparately (each with a comment) *The whole Text* (without a comment) was printed in one volume, in 1488. And the Text continued to be printed, as in thefe firft editions, fo in feveral others for 20 or 30 years, without marginal *Keri* or *Mafora*, and with greater agreement to the more antient MSS; till, about the year 1520, fome of the Jews adopted *later* MSS, and the *Mafora:* which abfurd preference has obtained ever fince.

In the laft Account I affured the Reader, that 108 *Tranfcripts* of Collations were then depofited in the Bodleian Library; and a Catalogue, fpecifying the Collations fo tranfcribed and depofited, was figned by the Principal Librarian, on *May* 2ᵈ.

* The place, where the latter of thefe 2 copies is preferved, was made known to me by my learned Friend Mr *Bruns*; whom I have defired to collate this *firft-printed* Pentateuch. And I was favoured with the notice of the former by the learned Monf. *Mercier*, the very worthy Librarian of the St *Genovefe* library at *Paris*; who has lately been prefented by His Moft Chriftian Majefty to a Mitred Abbey.

1767 : which Catalogue is too large to be inserted in this Account. And to the Transcripts before deposited have been lately added 21 ; so that the number, now in the Bodleian, amounts to ONE HUNDRED AND TWENTY NINE.

The only articles at home, which I shall here add, are — that I have been highly obliged by the reverend and learned Dr *Gill* ; who has extracted and sent me the Variations from the modern Bibles in the passages quoted in the *Talmuds* both of Jerusalem and Babylon, and also in the *Rabboth :* which Variations, in these antient books of the *Jews,* affect the Hebrew Text of the *Old* Testament, as the Variations in the antient *Christian* Fathers affect the Greek Text of the *New.* And lastly : the Hebrew MSS in England have been this year increased by Two, now my own ; which did belong to the late Dr *De Wilhem,* of *Lekkerkirk* near Rotterdam : and one of these is the magnificent and curious MS, which was celebrated in the Account of my Work for the year 1763. These MSS have been kindly purchased, at my request, by the Reverend Dr *Richardson,* Chaplain to His Excellency Sir JOSEPH YORKE, His Majesty's Ambassador at the *Hague.*

As to Collations procured, in the present year, from abroad ; I shall begin with those, which I have just received from DENMARK : very obligingly transmitted to me by His Excellency the Baron DE BERN-

BERNSTORFF, Principal Secretary of State. The Various Readings of *Seven* MSS, lately purchased in *Egypt*, must be thought very desirable. And therefore, when the use of these MSS was voluntarily offered me, by order of His late DANISH MAJESTY; I gratefully accepted it. And I now express my Thanks in this public manner to His Majesty the present KING OF DENMARK, not only for the use of these 7 MSS, but also of one other, long preserved in the Royal Library. These 8 MSS have been collated by the Oriental Professor Mr *Kall*, together with other learned Gentlemen at *Copenhagen*, the Professors *Cramer*, *Holmes*, *Rosenstand Goiske* &c.

I have likewise received a Collation of the whole Hebrew Bible, printed in 1494; which did belong to LUTHER, and is now preserved in the *Royal* Library at BERLIN. This curious edition was collated by the learned Professor *Schulze*, assisted by his learned Wife; and the Variations in this from the modern editions are very numerous and valuable. This Collation was very obligingly transmitted to me by His Excellency Sir ANDREW MITCHELL, His Majesty's Ambassador at *Berlin*.

From FLORENCE I have received this year the Collation of a MS in the Library of Duke STROZZI, collated by the learned Fathers *Berretta* and *Bartoli*; which Collation was kindly brought me by Mr

Worsely,

Worſely, at the requeſt of Sir HORACE MANN, His Majeſty's Reſident in that City.

The 2 MSS, formerly belonging to *Reuchlin*, now preſerved in the Library of *The Margrave of* BADEN-DURLAC (together with a 3d MS containing the book of *Pſalms*) have been examined, and their Variations ſent me, in the preſent year, by Mr *Bruns*. Theſe are the 2 MSS, from which, on account of their (ſuppoſed) very high antiquity and extraordinary merit, a new edition of the Hebrew Bible was propoſed to have been made about ten years ago. Their Various Readings are really of conſiderable value : and it is particularly obſervable, that in one of theſe MSS, after the prophecy of *Malachi*, the next book is *Daniel*; placed in that order by the Tranſcriber himſelf.

Among the learned Foreigners, by whom I have been favoured with Letters during this year, particular mention muſt be made of Profeſſor *Nagel*, of *Altdorff* near *Nuremberg*. From this Gentleman I have learnt, that an Hebrew Bible, in 7 folio volumes, which was lately to be ſold, is purchaſed for the public Library at Nuremberg. And this valuable MS, together with 3 others, is very fortunately preſerved in a Country, where there are Men ſo munificent, and animated with ſo much Public Spirit, as to order Collations of theſe MSS to be made for me AT THEIR OWN EXPENCE. The generous Perſons, who thus demonſtrate their

Zeal

Zeal for the honour of Revelation, and the common benefit of Europe, are *The Illustrious* CHRISTOPHER CHARLES KRESS DE KRESSENSTEIN, and *The Illustrious* PAUL CHARLES WELSER DE NEUNHOF; both *Knights of the holy Roman Empire*. To these Patrons the warmest Thanks, which I can express, are justly due; and their Examples, if followed, would render this Work compleat, by enabling it to appear at once, with the Various Readings of all the MSS in Europe. An Event this — which, though impossible upon the present Subscription, might very easily be obtained; if the RICH and the GREAT in the several parts of Europe would, at *their own Expence* likewise, order Collations to be made of the MSS in their respective Countries.

With the notice of this munificent offer from Nuremberg, must be again mentioned the liberal Subscription, with which my Work has been distinguished by THE ACADEMY OF MANNHEIM; a favour, already taken notice of with proper gratitude : and the *Continuance* of This Subscription is here acknowledged with great thankfulness.

Due mention has been also made of the favour of *Monf. L' Abbé Ladvocat*, late Hebrew Professor at *The Sorbonne*; who collated, *without reward*, several of the *Paris* MSS : and whose great zeal for the promotion of this Work appears farther from a Letter of his lately printed, in which are these
words

words — *mais nous n'aurons une edition pure et cor-rette du Texte Hébreu, que quand paroîtra celle que M. Kennicott Sçavant Anglois nous prepare. Je con-tribuerai de mon côté à l' aider dans cette importante entreprise, soit en lui communiquant mes remarques, soit en collationnant tous les Manuscrits Hébreux qui sont à Paris, et en lui en envoyant les Variantes.* *

Some of thefe Collations were fent me by the Pro-feffor himfelf ; and others, made under his care, have been (fince his death) kindly tranfmitted by *Monf. L'Abbé Le Blond :* from whom I have lately received the laft fruits of that Profeffor's benevo-lent affiftance. But my advantages from the *Sor-bonne* by no means ended with that Profeffor's life ; as he was fucceeded in the Hebrew Chair by my very learned Countryman *Monf. L'Abbé Hooke,* to whom I am under ftill greater obligations. For thro' his favour, and the kindnefs of *Monf. L'Abbé Affeline,* I have received feveral other Collations, partly from the Sorbonne, and partly from the

---

* A learned Proteftant alfo, Profeffor *Verfchuir,* of *Frane-quer,* in his Differtation lately printed, has honoured my Work with the following approbation. *De eo nobis et univerfo orbi Chriftiano gratulamur, quod tot manu exarati codices remarfe-rint, ex quorum collatione genuinæ lectiones a peritis et veri aman-tibus criticis magnam partem facilè indagari poffint ; et quod iftum laborem in fe fufceperit B. Kennicotus, vir — a quo optima quævis de hoc opere fperamus —— publicè pro fufcepto hoc utiliffimo opere maximas ago gratias ; atque ut id ad finem perducere conetur, enixè rogo.*

Royal

Royal Library at Paris; and the affiftance of thefe Gentlemen is obligingly offered, and gratefully accepted, as to fome other MSS.

My thanks however are not due to thefe two Friends, merely for fome Collations; but alfo, for a thoufand Obligations which they conferred upon me, in perfon, whilft I was at P A R I S, vifiting the MSS, during the laft fummer. For, convinced of its being my duty to do every thing in my power towards the perfection of my Work, and convinced likewife that many advantages would refult from *my own* examinations, in a City, which may boaft of near *One Hundred* Hebrew and Samaritan MSS; I went, and examined accordingly : and I have the pleafure to acquaint the Reader, that the Vifit has been productive of very great utility to my Work, in various ways. And I here acknowledge, with the warmeft gratitude, the many Favours fhewn to me at Paris, in the moft honourable manner; particularly, by His Grace THE DUKE DE NIVER-NOIS, and His Excellency THE EARL OF ROCH-FORD. To which Illuftrious Names I muft add that of His Grace The Lord ARCH-BISHOP OF PARIS; who very obligingly ordered feveral Libraries to be examined, where there might poffibly be Hebrew MSS not publickly known : and has fince condefcended to favour me with a Letter, expreffive of His great Goodwill to me and to my Work.

The

The ufe of the 37 Hebrew MSS, and 2 Samaritan, preferved in the very magnificent Library of
His Most Christian Majesty, was granted
me, in the moft obliging manner, by the Royal
Librarians *Monf. Caperonier* and *Monf. Bejot.* One
of the oldeft and beft of thefe Royal MSS, containing *the whole Bible*, has been examined; and
the Various Readings, extracted from it, are numerous and of great confequence. The treafures
of the Sorbonne were freely opened to me likewife; in which ample library are 29 Hebrew MSS.
The fame favour was obtained from the learned
Fathers of the Oratory, as to their 8 Hebrew
MSS, and 2 Samaritan; one of thefe is the copy
from which *Morinus* printed, and is the only Samaritan MS (out of 16 now in Europe) which has
yet been made proper ufe of: though the other 4
copies in *Paris* have the true readings in feveral
places, where the MS of *Morinus* is wrong. The
Librarians alfo of St Genovefe, St Germain
des Pres, St Victoire, and the Minim
Fathers, very readily communicated their MSS:
in the 3d and 4th of which libraries are 2 Hebrew
MSS; in the 2d library are 3 Hebrew MSS and
4 of the Greek Verfion, one of which is above a
thoufand years old; and in the 1ft library is one
Hebrew MS, with a MS of the *Samaritan* Pentateuch: and, as I found the Samaritan MS to contain *many and valuable* Various Readings, it has
been fince collated for me by my learned Friend

Mr

Mr *Lobstein* of *Strasburg*. From this same excellent
library was lent me also a written Collation (made
by *Morinus*) of the Samaritan and Hebrew Penta-
teuchs; noting their differences, and frequently
adding the authorities of the antient Versions:
which curious MS was transcribed for me, while
at Paris, by Mr *Bruns*, who kindly came to me
thither from *Carlsruhe*. As the MSS beforementioned were, out of singular Veneration for my
Work, lent me at my own Hôtel; and as I had
therefore *all the Samaritan MSS at Paris open before
me at the same time:* I not only was honoured with
a Sight, which perhaps no other person ever saw;
but I also felt a peculiar pleasure, at beholding
these precious remains of sacred Antiquity, which
I hoped to render very serviceable to the correction
of the Hebrew Pentateuch.

Among the many learned and worthy Persons,
who contributed to render my stay at Paris useful
and agreeable; my Thanks are particularly due to
Monf. DE BREQUIGNY, Monf. DE BEAUMONT,
Father BERTIER, and Colonel DROMGOLD. And
lastly: I must make my public acknowledgments
to The President and Members of THE ROYAL
ACADEMY OF INSCRIPTIONS AND BELLES
LETTRES, for the great Honour done me by
admitting me a Member of their Illustrious Society; which Admission is expressed in the following
Diploma.

Q   *Extrait*

Extrait des Regiſtres de l' ACADEMIE ROYALE *des* INSCRIPTIONS & BELLES LETTRES.

Du Vendredi, Sept Août, 1767.

Sur la propoſition faite à la Compagnie par M. Le Préſident de donner un témoignage public d'eſtime & de conſideration à M. Le Docteur Kennicot, qui s'eſt fait un nom dans la Republique des Lettres par des ouvrages où l'erudition et la critique ſe font également remarquer, La Compagnie perſuadée qu'il eſt de ſon devoir et de ſon intérêt, d'entretenir avec les ſçavants étrangers un commerce utile au progrés des Lettres, a, par une déliberation unanime, mis Monſieur Le Docteur Kennicot au nombre de ſes correſpondants, et a chargé M. Le Beau, ſon Secretaire perpetuel, de lui expédier des Lettres de Correſpondance ſuivant l'uſage et dans la forme ordinaire.

En foi de quoi J'ai ſigné les preſentes Lettres ſcellées du ſçeau de l'Academie. Fait à Paris au Louvre le dit jour ſept Août, 1767.

LE BEAU, *Secretaire Perpetuel.*

As this Year has been diſtinguiſhed by two Events, not already mentioned; I cannot cloſe this Account, without making the moſt grateful mention of Both. The one is — the Honour done me by His Grace The Lord ARCH-BISHOP OF CANTERBURY, and The other GREAT OFFICERS

OF

OF STATE &c. who are Electors of The RAD-
CLIFFE Librarian, in appointing me lately to that
Office. And the other article, with which I shall
conclude this Account, is — my great Obligation
to a Lady lately deceased, whom I had never seen;
Mrs ELIZABETH GRIFFEN, of *Wokingham, Berks*:
who, from the opinion She had formed of the Use-
fulness of my Work, and of the Labour with which
it is attended, has bequeathed to me by Her Will
a Legacy of TWO HUNDRED POUNDS; to be paid
by Her Executors, *as soon as I shall have compleated*
the Collation of the Holy Bible, which I have now
undertaken.

THE CERTIFICATE

from

The Royal Professor of Hebrew,

nearly the same as before,

see in page 109.

ACCOUNT IX.

At the End of the Year 1768.

IN the profecution of a Work fo very laborious, as that of collating *all* the MSS of the Hebrew Bible in our own country, and procuring collations of the beft MSS abroad (which was at firft thought to require *Ten Years* to perfect it) I am truly thankful to DIVINE PROVIDENCE, that I have been fo far blefled with Health, as to fee the Work advance to the end of the *Ninth* year, with a fair profpect of its being compleated in the year following.

Before I enter into the particulars of this year's Progrefs, I muft exprefs myfelf moft gratefully for *the Illuftrious Patronage*, with which it is ftill honoured; and for *the Public-fpirited Subfcription*, by which it has been, for fo many years, fingularly fupported: an acknowledgment, which is the more neceflary at this time, becaufe the Subfcription in this *Ninth* year is greater than in any year preceding. And I am very happy in feeing, that the opinion of the Learned is more and more favourable to a Work ; which indeed I find to be of

greater

greater and greater confequence, in proportion as more MSS, and alfo more printed Editions, are examined for the Benefit of it.

To the number of 85 MSS at home, before collated, are to be now added 15; fo that the whole number of our own MSS, thus far collated, amounts to ONE HUNDRED. Of thefe 15 MSS, 2 belong to *The Mafter and Fellows of St John's Col-lege, in Cambridge*; 1 to the Rev. Dr *Barton*, War-den of *Merton* College; and 1 to the Rev. Mr *Price*, the Bodley Librarian: and for the ufe of thefe 4 MSS, I defire thefe Gentlemen to accept my public thanks. Another of thefe MSS was pre-fented to me by the Rev. Dr *Hunt*, our celebrated Hebrew Profeffor; whofe Favour to this Work, and its author, cannot be fufficiently acknowledged.

But what has added fuperior luftre to the Work, in the prefent year, is a MS, which I have lately had the honour to purchafe for the Royal Library, by the command of HIS MAJESTY, the Supreme and Munificent Patron of this Work. This curious MS, which contains the whole He-brew Bible, has alfo been collated; and it has one pre-eminence above every other MS I have feen — that it belonged, not only to a SYNAGOGUE (tho' even that circumftance would have been im-portant, as it contains a multitude of Variations) but to a Synagogue in JERUSALEM itfelf. For a very celebrated Rabbi, who was born in Spain

in

in 1194, built a Synagogue at Jerufalem ; and in this Synagogue, (which was built about 500 years fince) was this MS (which was written about 400 years fince) preferved with the utmoft veneration, till Jerufalem was taken by the Emperor *Selim* in 1517. The MS was then feized by a Turkifh Officer, who carried it to Aleppo ; where, in 1683, it came into the hands of the celebrated *D'Arvieux:* and it was afterwards purchafed by an Englifh Gentleman, who brought it home to enrich his own country. In this MS the *Pfalms*, *Job*, and *Proverbs*, are written in *Hemiftics* ; as the Hebrew Poetry certainly fhould be. And, tho' it has fuffered by rafures, it has ftill many various Readings, and feveral of confequence : in particular, it has *Two Verfes* in one place, which are clearly genuine, tho' the Mafora has pronounced them fpurious.

In the laft Annual Account it was mentioned, that 129 *Tranfcripts* were then depofited in the Bodleian ; and this number is now made 143, by 14 other Tranfcripts, added lately : for which the Principal Librarian has given his Receipt, as ufual.

As to Foreign MSS, I fhall firft mention thofe, which are preferved in the *Royal* Library at *Copenhagen :* of which MSS 8 have been collated, and the collations of them received, as mentioned in the account of laft year. And here I acknowledge, with the warmeft gratitude, the Honour of a Promife from His Majefty THE KING OF DENMARK, (at the recommendation of my Friend His Excellency *The Count de Bernstorff*) that not only these 3 MSS, but also every other in the Royal Library, containing any part of the Hebrew Bible, shall be sent to *England*, for my own personal inspection.

To the collation of 7 MSS, before received from the Ambrosian Library at *Milan*, are to be now added 5 more; finished by the care of *Henrico A Porta*, the celebrated Professor of the Oriental Languages at *Pavia*; and the learned Dr *Baptista Branca*, the Ambrosian Librarian: which Collations were very obligingly brought to England lately by Mr *Stewart*, at the request of His Excellency *Sir Horatio Mann*, His Majesty's Resident at *Florence*.

Thro' the care of *William Norton Esq*, His Majesty's Minister at *Berne*, I have lately received, from the celebrated Professor *Breitinger*, the collation of a valuable MS of the Hebrew Bible preserved at *Zuric*.

From *Berlin* I have this year received a collation of the third part of that MS, which is the most considerable in the Royal Library of His Majesty THE KING OF PRUSSIA. And there being at *Brieg* in *Silesia* an Hebrew MS, represented by Wolfius, as having very many Variations; I have engaged for a complete collation of it.

I have lately been favoured with a Letter from M. *Obelin*, Public Librarian at *Strasburg*; who has,

in

in a very obliging manner, offered to send me the Variations of the MSS preserved in that valuable Library : of which MSS he has given me a very particular account, together with a curious specimen of their various readings. The other Libraries at *Strasburg* are now under examination, as to their Hebrew MSS, by my worthy friend Mr *Lobstein*; in consequence of Letters recommendatory from *The Lord* ARCH-BISHOP *of* PARIS: and I am signally obliged to His Grace for fresh assurances of His Zeal for this Work, expressed in a Letter which I have not long since had the Honour to receive from Him.

As it has been repeatedly proved, that the MSS at *Erfurt*, which were made use of for Michaelis's edition of the Hebrew Bible at *Hall*, in 1720, contain Variations much more numerous and important than are inserted in that edition ; I have lately desired, that a new and compleat collation may be made of the oldest and best of these MSS.

While these several collations are making for this Work, with other collations not before-mentioned ; particularly at *Nuremberg* by Professor *Nagel*, at the Expence of the Illustrious C. C. KRESS *de Kressenstein*, and the Illustrious P. C. WELSER *de Neunhof*; and at *Paris*, by the free services of my very learned Friend *Monf. L'Abbé Asseline*, Dr and Professor of the *Sorbonne*; and while every other attempt in my power has been made, towards en-
riching

*r*iching this Work from the various Countries of EUROPE : other parts of the World (how great foever the difficulties of enquiry there, and however unpromifing the profpect) have not been unattended to.

My Friend General *Melvill*, whom I had requefted to examine in AMERICA, has lately affured me, that, after many enquiries, he could hear of no Hebrew MSS there, but what were very modern. AFRICA has largely contributed towards the prefent Work ; particularly, by the MSS purchafed in *Cairo* at the command of His Majefty The late KING OF DENMARK. At *Conftantinople* a curious MS was purchafed, and has been kindly prefented to me, by His Excellency Sir *James Porter*. And if we pafs from thence into ASIA ; there even *Jerufalem* itfelf has furnifhed a compleat MS, which has been already celebrated, and belongs now to *The Royal Library* in Great Britain.

Much has been reported, concerning Hebrew MSS preferved in *China* ; particularly, at *Cai-fong-fu*. And as the leaft poffibility of procuring fomething, either MS itfelf, or Collation of a MS, from that very diftant part of the Globe, was fufficient to engage my earneft attention ; I have been lately enabled to fend thither a Commiffion, either for purchafing a MS, or procuring fome Collation : for which latter purpofe I have alfo fent to *Canton* a printed Hebrew Bible. And for the

R   oppor-

opportunity of making this attempt I am exceedingly obliged to *Frederick Pigou*, Efq; whom I defire to accept my public acknowledgments for his very benevolent affiftance.

I fhall clofe this Annual Account with one article of intelligence ; which I have referved for the laft, becaufe it is the moft important. The very *firft* edition of the Hebrew Bible, printed in 1488, and fortunately purchafed by my Friend Mr *Sanford* (as mentioned in the laft Annual Account) has been now compleatly collated with the edition of *Van. Hooght*, in 1705 ; and the Variations between thefe editions (the former printed more agreeably to the oldeft and beft MSS, and the latter to the lateft and worft) have been carefully computed. And now, to the great Surprize of the Learned through Europe — of thofe, who acknowledged fome differences and corruptions in the *printed* copies — as well as of thofe, who infifted on their abfolute agreement and integrity — I fay, to the Surprize of the Learned univerfally, I acquaint them, that the Words, which here vary either in the Whole or in fome Part, amount to above

TWELVE THOUSAND!

Now from this Difcovery arife the following very interefting Queftions. How are we to determine between thefe 2. Editions, in thefe 12000 inftances ? Are we, without any reafon, to prefer either Edition *univerfally* ; or to prefer *fometimes* the

the one, *sometimes* the other? If neither, without
a reason; what reason can there be so good, as
The Concurrence of MSS? And if the Authority
of *MSS* (together with that of the antient Versions,
Context &c.) is to determine; does not this de-
monstrate — I will not say, the great *Expediency*,
but — the absolute N E C E S S I T Y of collating such
MSS, that so the Learned may judge, the more
safely, between these printed Editions of a Book,
which is of such vast Importance? If, then, the
N E C E S S I T Y of this Work be certain; how
grateful ought the Public to be, and Posterity will
be for ages to come, to A L L   T H O S E, who have
patronized a Work so very beneficial to Mankind!

If the Work, thus in every year confirmed by
more and stronger Authorities, and thus supported
with encreasing Zeal by the Generosity of the Public, shall be published by the person, who has thus
far conducted it; if *he shall live* to introduce to
the World the result of all these Sacred Enquiries:
the grateful Dedication of his Work to A L L   I T S
P A T R O N S will form a very pleasing part of his
Duty, in that Publication. At present; the whole
in his power is, to publish annually, with his warmest
Thanks, the Names of T H E   S U B S C R I B E R S:
and the Catalogue of Them for this Year is given,
as usual, after the following Certificate.

THE CERTIFICATE.

THE Delegates of the Prefs, in the Univerfity of Oxford, having in January 1760 fubfcribed to Dr Kennicott's Collation of the Hebrew MSS; and having inferted in an Order then made the following words [*That their Subfcription be continued at the beginning of every Year, upon Dr Kennicott's producing a Certificate from the Royal Profeffor of Hebrew, that in his Judgment Dr Kennicott hath made a competent Progrefs in the faid Work during the Year preceding*;] and the faid Delegates, as well as the Univefity of Cambridge, having in the beginning of the prefent Year again renewed their Subfcription to this Work on condition of a Certificate from me, as before-mentioned ; and Dr Kennicott having applied to me for fuch a Certificate : I do hereby accordingly Certify, for the Satisfaction of both thefe Univerfities, and of fuch Perfons as have encouraged this Work by their Subfcriptions, that the feveral Parts of the Collation, made during this Ninth Year, have been laid before me ; and my Opinion is, that Dr Kennicott hath made a very competent Progrefs in the faid Collation. Upon confidering feveral of the Various Readings, which he has already difcovered in the Hebrew MSS ; I think this Work will be of very confiderable Service to Sacred Literature. And as the Work appears to be of greater and greater confequence, in proportion as more MSS are collated ; I cannot but take this opportunity of congratulating the Patrons of it, on its being now fo far advanced, and brought fo near to a Conclufion.

THO. HUNT,

Chrift-Church;
Decemb. 30, 1760.

Regius Profeffor of Hebrew.

Account X;

At the End of the Year 1769:

Concluding

The Whole Work.

WHEN I undertook the Collation of the Hebrew MSS of the Old Teſtament, my mind was greatly affected with very different conſiderations ; ſome of which it may not be improper to ſtate here, when I am about to acquaint the Public with the Conclusion of this Undertaking.

The certain Importance of this Work to *The Public* — the poſſible conſequences of it to *myſelf*, in various ways ; particularly, as to the Injury which my Conſtitution would probably ſuffer, from the Labour and very cloſe Application neceſſary for many Years — the *Exhortations* of thoſe, who zealouſly recommended it — and the Diſpoſition of others to *cenſure* both the Work itſelf, and the Method of conducting it, be that Method whatever it would — furniſhed out a multitude of reflections, and topics of very diſagreeable as well as agreeable poſſibility.

poſſibility. Some of theſe circumſtances would perhaps have induced any man, not bleſſed with uncommon Health (as I then was) to tremble and decline the Taſk ; and yet other conſiderations, particularly that of devoting the moſt uſeful part of life to the nobleſt purpoſe, prevailed with me at laſt to undertake it.

THE BIBLE had ever appeared to me a Book of infinite conſequence to myſelf and the reſt of Mankind ; and I conſidered it as a Gift worthy of GOD, and worthy of all human acceptation. The many Difficulties, formerly occurring in the peruſal of it, I had uſually attributed to my own Ignorance, particularly of the Original Text, and to the Want of Exactneſs in our Engliſh Tranſlation.

When I learnt the Hebrew language, and for ſome years afterwards ; I was of the ſame opinion with moſt Divines, that *every Word and Letter in the printed Hebrew Text was pure and genuine.* I therefore concluded, that neither the real Obſcurities, nor the apparent Inconſiſtencies, were at all chargeable to the Inaccuracy of Tranſcribers ; and of courſe, that a Remedy was not to be ſought, or would be ſought to no good purpoſe, in any attempt to correct the printed Hebrew Text.

However, being diſpoſed to give up even this opinion, if it was found wrong, I became afterwards convinced of my Miſtake ; and when convinced

vinced upon evidence, which feemed abundantly
fatisfactory, I thought it my duty to endeavour to
convince others. I ventured accordingly to publifh
my Reafons. And, in order to awaken others to
a juft fenfe of the *true* State of the *Old Teftament*;
I produced fuch parts of it, as were either not to
be explained by themfelves, or not to be rendered
confiftent with other parts, without allowing ——
that *the prefent Text is much corrupted.* And at the
fame time, that the Diforder was pointed out, a
Remedy was prefcribed; or rather, was difcovered.
For I found upon enquiry, that there were in England very many facred Hebrew MSS, at that time
quite undifturbed, at leaft not at all made ufe of.
And in thefe MSS I found more than fufficient
proofs of the Fallibility of Jewifh Tranfcribers, in
general; and alfo fome of thofe particular readings,
which, tho' different from the printed Text, I had
before fet down as true.

Such a Difcovery as this — of MSS, containing
the whole or parts of a Book moft juftly venerable
— and thefe MSS, very many in number — and
MSS, which had never been attended to, though
they contained Thoufands of Variations; many of
which were of real confequence to the Honour of
R E V E L A T I O N — fuch a Difcovery could not
but engage the attention of thofe, who were at all
friends to Learning and to Religion. This was indeed the confequence. But then, while the Learned
were thankful, and much pleafed with the happy
confe-

confequences likely to refult from correcting the miftakes in our printed Heb. Bible; fome thought it right to vilify the man, who thus offered his Difcovery; reflecting on him illiberally and very abfurdly, *for writing* (as they called it) *againft the word of God.*

Now, though Abufe, from men of zeal without knowledge, is the reverfe of difgrace; it was ftill more honourable to receive Approbation from Men eminent for Literature and Piety, and diftinguifhed alfo by their Rank in Life. And, being animated by fuch Friends as Thefe to purfue the fame en-quiries, after publifhing *One Differtation* on this fubject, I fpent Six Years in preparing and pub-lifhing a *Second*; which, at the fame time that it proved more fully the Expediency of examining Hebrew MSS, gave notice of many other fuch MSS, worthy of examination.

But, though I endeavoured as much as poffible to recommend a Collation of thefe MSS, yet I did not mean to recommend *myfelf* for the Collator; or indeed as any one of thofe, who poffibly might be prevailed upon to undertake a Work of fuch vaft fatigue. Having, however, been applied to by the Delegates of our Univerfity-Prefs, to whom *the Royal Profeffor of Hebrew* had recommended me; and having been repeatedly and earneftly exhorted to it by fo Great a Perfon as The late A R C H-B I S H O P of C A N T E R B U R Y: I, at laft, in the begin-

beginning of the year 1760, told His Grace, that I confented; and that I was refolved to apply myfelf wholly to this Employment — provided, *it was made prudent for me in point of Circumftances.* And as I forefaw, that great Encouragement would be granted to *the Work,* which indeed has fince proved much greater than I expected; fo I made no doubt, but a generous Attention would be fhewn to *the perfon undertaking it :* who thus neglected every other purfuit, for the fake of this one; and who was thus deftined to grow old, in the Service of the Public.

That the Work, thus entered upon, might not appear romantic and impracticable; and be deemed either impoffible, or unlikely, to be brought to a conclufion, at leaft during the lives of thofe who fo much wifhed the performance of it; it feemed right to confine the Work to *fuch MSS, as were preferved, and the ufe of which could be obtained, in our own Country :* with the declared intention of procuring (during that interval) Collations of as many of the beft *Foreign* MSS, as *Time* and *Expence* would allow.

After the moft exact calculation I was capable of making, I publifhed my opinion — that the Collation, thus undertaken, would probably be finifhed in TEN YEARS. And how long foever fuch a Time might then, and may ftill, appear to men, not much acquainted with the nature of this Work;

S yet

yet thofe, who can eftimate the comparing of a
printed copy, *Letter after Letter*, with *every Word*
of *every Chapter*, in O N E H U N D R E D A N D
F O R T Y Hebrew MSS, will perhaps be aftonifhed,
that *Twenty* Years were not found neceffary, inftead
of *Ten*. Efpecially, when it is added — that every
fuch Collation, containing its whole catalogue of
Omiffions, *Additions*, *Tranfpofitions* &c, with all its
marks of *Rafures* &c, (fee pag. 35 — 43) was to
be tranfcribed ; and either the original Collation,
or its Tranfcript, depofited in the Bodleian library.
And this confiderable addition of labour was ftill
further increafed, at my own choice ; becaufe I
thought it right (though this was not required)
that Copies of all the *Foreign* Collations fhould be
taken, and depofited, likewife.

The Account, publifhed at the end of the year
1768, mentioned, that *One Hundred* of our own
Hebrew MSS were then collated. And I have
now the pleafure to acquaint the Public, that *the
Whole Remainder of our own MSS* (i. e. all, which
I could difcover, and obtain the ufe of) *are now
collated likewife*. So that, on ftating this Account,
which concludes the T E N T H Year, I find myfelf
intitled to one comfortable reflection, feldom if
ever due to Public Undertakers of any kind, that
of having ftrictly kept my word, and finifhing exactly
at the time which I had named *near Ten Years ago*.
And this circumftance is, I confefs, not the lefs
agreeable, becaufe it will mortify fome men of
little

little minds; who (whether from envy, or malice, or whatever other evil principle) have been known to infinuate — that, *no doubt, the Undertaker of this Work, having it in his power to be fecret in the Management of his Collation, would take care to protract it fo prudently, as to make it a good Settlement for Life.* How far this benevolent intimation may have been juftly grounded, will appear more clearly at *the conclufion* of this Account. For from thence the Reader will be better qualified to judge —— Whether the Undertaker of this Work has, or has not, acted in the profecution of it, with as much *Difinterestednefs*, or at leaft with as much Zeal for *his Work and the Public*, as the Public, however generous, have fhewn for *his Work and him.*

As to the preceding calculation of Ten Years, it fhould be obferved, that fo much time was fuppofed neceffary for examining only the *Manufcripts* of the Hebrew Bible; and fuch only of thofe MSS, as were *then difcovered:* feveral others having been fince found, and collated, likewife. And as to the *printed* Editions; a collation of *Them* was not at firft judged to be at all neceffary. So very nearly, or rather fo exactly, had thefe been all thought to agree, excepting the fingle edition of the *Hagiographa* in 1487; that the collation of no printed Edition, excepting that one, was at firft intended.

But,

But, how greatly has this Work been extended, beyond the firſt idea of it ! — not only by the addition of ſeveral other MSS — but alſo, by the addition of *Six* printed Editions of the *Whole* Old Teſtament ; and of *Six* printed Editions of very large *Parts* of it : for in theſe *Twelve* Editions are contained near ONE HUNDRED AND SIXTY SIX THOUSAND Verſes. And here, if any one ſhould be diſpoſed to look back upon the term of *Ten Years* ; and pleaſantly remark the wonderful *Exactneſs* of that Calculation, which required juſt ſo much time merely for the MSS, or rather for a part of them ; and yet could find room alſo for ſuch very large Additions : I would ſuggeſt to ſuch remarker — that my Expedition did in part depend on the Number of my Aſſiſtants — that as the Work increaſed, ſo did the Subſcription to it — and therefore, being enabled to employ more Aſſiſtants, I choſe to do ſo ; in order, that not one ſingle Year's Subſcription ſhould be occaſioned by the Collation, beyond what was computed originally.

The very numerous and intereſting Variations in ſo many *printed Editions*, eſpecially the oldeſt, as it was a kind of evidence totally unexpected, ſo was it the more welcome, for appearing when a Collation of the *MSS* was far advanced. The Work had before, while reſting on the many differences in the *MSS*, been recommended only on the point

of

of EXPEDIENCY; but, when supported also by
the many differences in the *printed* copies, was, as
it demanded to be, urged and pressed more strongly,
as a matter of NECESSITY. And indeed those,
who have marked with careful attention the rise
and progress of this Work, must have seen with
perhaps singular surprize — how, new light and
fresh evidence have arisen, in the several stages of
it! As if certain parts of the compleat Discovery
had been reserved, occasionally to answer these two
purposes; to re-invigorate the Mind, when almost
sinking under the labours of enquiry: and to in-
spire the Patrons of the Work (as it did the far
greater part of them) with such an increasing conviction of it's moment, that, so far from being
weary with well-doing, they seemed to contribute
with the more zeal, the longer they contributed.

It may here be useful, and not unentertaining,
to bring together the several points in question,
relative to this Work; with a Confutation of each
Objection, made to it: as such a *Juxta-position* will
render the whole Matter much more clear, and
carry with it more full Conviction.

Case the FIRST. About 20 years since I attempted a correction of some errors in the printed
Hebrew Text, by comparing 2 parallel Chapters;
in doing which, the only helps, besides the great
advantages of that *Parallelism*, were the *Context*
and the *Antient Versions*. But here it was easy to
objeςt,

object, that *a scheme of correction, formed upon these principles, would have been much more satisfactory, had there been any Hebrew MSS, which confirmed any of these emendations.* The force of this objection is granted; and it was actually foreseen. MSS therefore were sought after, and found; by which several of these corrections, before made, were actually confirmed.

Objection 2. B u t, *how could the Antient Versions support any alteration of the Hebrew Text? — when they are bad Paraphrases rather than good Versions: because none of their numerous and great differences from our Hebrew Text are at all countenanced by Hebrew MSS.* Thus had men long affirmed, without the least proof; indeed, in a matter totally unexamined: and in defiance of the strongest proofs to the contrary, at that very time extant in the MSS themselves. For in those MSS, which I at first discovered, I soon met with several readings, entirely different from the printed Hebrew copies; and exactly agreeing with the Greek, Syriac, and other Antient Versions.

3. B u t, *as the MSS, thus discovered, were not many; perhaps these would have been contradicted, or invalidated, by other MSS in England, or by MSS in Foreign countries.* The very contrary was expected, as the result of further enquiry. Further enquiry was made, and other MSS were found at home; and upon enquiries also abroad, many MSS were found

found there likewife : almoft every one of them proving the *Fallibility* of its Tranfcriber, and many of them confirming ftill more amply the authority of the *Antient Verfions*.

4. B u t, *whatever be the condition of thefe MSS ; yet are they, when taken all together, but very few, compared with the printed Editions.* So far from thefe MSS being few, they amount to about 500. My firft Differtation fpecified 70, in our own Country ; where I have fince difcovered as many more. And if I fhould add about 90, which I have feen in *France*, together with thofe fent to me at Oxford from other Foreign parts ; the whole number, which I myfelf have feen, and in part examined, amounts to about 250 — half the number of the whole, known at prefent in Europe. In the fcale, oppofite to all thefe MSS, are to be now put our *modern* printed editions ; which, as they are almoft all taken from the edition of *Ben Chaim*, in 1525, are reducible in point of authority nearly to *that one* edition. The *oldeft editions*, which were printed on a very different plan (*i. e.* not from MSS *the moft perfectly* Maforetical, which were the *lateft*, but from MSS *the leaft* Maforetical, which were the *oldeft*) are now very fcarce and uncommon ; and indeed thefe fall not within the force of this objection.

5. B u t, *however numerous the MSS, now extant, may be ; they are all late and modern : therefore not*

to be compared with thofe ufed by the Maforetic Doc-
tors, above 1000 *years ago* ; *and from thefe MSS
was our Text taken.* MSS, of 600, 700 and 800
years of age, are certainly not modern ; and to
this antiquity may feveral of thefe MSS fairly pre-
tend. A MS, not more than 600 years old, is of
refpectable antiquity ; efpecially, when compared
with one of 400 or 300 : and it is from MSS of
thefe later dates, that our *common printed Editions*
have been derived. The Editions muft agree with
the MSS, from which they have been taken. The
modern Editions agree, and they agree only, with
the *lateft* and *worft* MSS ; whereas the older the
MSS are, the more they vary from the modern
Editions, and vary almoft univerfally for the better.

6. B u t, *as the Chaldee Paraphrafe was taken
from MSS near the time of Chrift* ; *and as that Paraphrafe agrees with the modern Hebrew Bibles, in many
of the places charged with late corruption : fuch
places are certainly uncorrupted.* This objection,
which has a plaufible appearance at firft, will immediately vanifh ; when it is obferved, that the
modern Chaldee Paraphrafe is (for it has been
proved from Chaldee MSS — fee my Second Differtation, pag. 177 &c:) *wilfully altered,* in feveral places, to make it agree with the modern Hebrew Text.

7. B u t, *as the Samaritan Pentateuch is fo noto-
rioufly corrupted* ; *the Hebrew Text muft be preferred,*
wherever

wherever it differs from the Samaritan. There are indeed many grofs errors in the Samaritan Pentateuch, as it is printed in the *London* Polyglott (an edition *in general* highly excellent and meritorious) but then *the Samaritan MSS* are free from, and will therefore correct, thefe errors. And indeed the Samaritan Pentateuch fhould, in my opinion, be held very precious ; becaufe I apprehend, that fome places in the *Hebrew* Pentateuch will never be intelligible, nor others ever become defenfible, till corrected agreeably to the Samaritan. And it is very material to obferve, that the older even the *Hebrew* MSS are, the more they agree with the Samaritan. Of the Samaritan Pentateuch I have feen TWELVE MSS : only *Sixteen* are now known in Europe ; and, of thefe, *Eight* are collated for my Work already. As to this Pentateuch, fee alfo the preceding pages 56 and 57.

8. BUT, *any fond hopes of great matters from Hebrew MSS muft be ill-grounded : the trial has been made, and publifhed ; for 5 MSS, at Erfurt, were felected to adorn the Hebrew Bible printed by Michaelis, at Hall, in 1720 ; and the various readings, therein exhibited from thefe MSS, are fo few, and thefe few fo trifling, that it is a wonder how the Collators could fo weary themfelves for very vanity !* This would indeed be a little difcouraging, if it were really fact. But the truth is, that thefe MSS have been ftrangely mifreprefented, in that edition ; and that they contain important Variations, which were

T   not

not fuffered to appear in that Bible. For the learned
Editor, being *a devotee to the Mafora*, publifhed
fuch Variations only, as would not difgrace the
Text Maforetically now eftablifhed. The proof of
this important article has been already mentioned,
in page 86. But I cannot again mention this Difcovery, without celebrating that very ingenuous
candour, and that ardent love of truth (fuperior
to every *Family* confideration) which rendered my
very learned Friend Profeffor M i c h a e l i s, not
only zealous to find out the real fact, but alfo ready
to communicate it.

9. B u t, *all thefe Hebrew MSS, now fo pompoufly
recommended, are fpurious, and full of Faults; and
were fold by Jews to Chriftians, becaufe not worthy
of admiffion into the Synagogues.* — So eafy a thing
it is, to affirm roundly, without the leaft fhadow
of proof! If indeed it be a crime to differ from
the printed copies, in having readings more agreeable to the *Context*, more agreeable to the *Antient
Verfions*, and more agreeable to the *New Teftament*;
then muft thefe MSS, efpecially the older of them,
plead *Guilty:* otherwife, every fuch Variation ex-
alts *their* Honour, and encreafes *our* Obligation.
Some of thefe MSS were written by renowned
Rabbies; and others, for the ufe, or at the command, of their Princes and Great Men. There is
one, above 550 years old, written in the days of
Rabbi Solomon Jarchi, and therefore probably by
that famous Rabbi *himfelf*, becaufe it contains his
                                        Commentary;

Commentary; in which MS are many and valuable
Variations. And I have found many and valuable
Variations, in another MS; which did belong to
a *Synagogue*, and to a Synagogue in *Jerusalem* itself;
which was preserved there, as very precious and
very venerable : but it now belongs to the magnificent Library of His Majesty THE KING OF
GREAT BRITAIN. See a further account of
this curious MS, already given in page 125.

10. BUT, *as all the Printed copies, in whatever*
part of the World printed, have very nearly, if not
absolutely, the same Text; that Text, thus uniformly
established, must have been taken from MSS better,
and more to be depended on, than those now produced
with such very strange Variations. What is here
supposed, or rather taken for granted, has lately
been found, not only to be without foundation,
but also to be the very reverse of the truth ; because
some of the printed Editions differ from others, as
much as the MSS do from the printed Editions,
and from one another. One only, which is the
very first edition of the whole Hebrew Bible,
printed in 1488, has more than 12000 Variations
from the Text, as now commonly printed ; very
many of which Variations greatly affect the Sense.
See this Edition further celebrated, in the preceding pages 112 and 130.

Lastly. BUT, *as this one may be the only printed*
Edition, which has many and great Variations, it may

have

have been taken from a very bad MS. The perad-
ventures, in this laſt objection, can prove nothing.
And how feeble and vain are Conjectures, when
confronted by real Facts ! The edition of the *Hagiographa,* printed in 1487, and that of the whole
Bible, printed in 1494, having alſo been collated
for this Work, are found to contain Thouſands of
Variations ; many of which are of indiſputable importance. And yet, theſe two Editions differ ſo
much from each other, and from that of 1488, as
to prove, that they were not printed from one another. See theſe editions of 1487, and 1494,
mentioned before, in pages 101 — 104.

In conſequence of the Diſcovery laſt mentioned,
and of the ſeveral other Diſcoveries ſpecified in the
articles preceding, it follows, with the force of
Demonſtration — that *a careful Collation of the beſt
Hebrew MSS, and of the oldeſt printed Editions, is*
T H E M E T H O D *abſolutely neceſſary to be taken, in
order to the forming of a proper judgment, concerning
the Hebrew Text of the Old Teſtament.* And therefore, ſince we have now ſeen the various Objec-
tions, attended with their ſeveral Confutations ;
ſince we have been witneſſes to the laſt breathings
of a dying Opinion, concerning the Integrity of
what is greatly corrupted ; and ſince the abſolute
Neceſſity of ſuch a Collation, as I have undertaken,
is at laſt proved to univerſal Satisfaction : I cannot
but congratulate the Public, on this Collation being
now completed.

But

But it is by no means my prefent intention to wait upon The Subscribers to this Work, only with this general notice, that *The Collation is now finished*. They will receive pleafure from fome particulars, which have diftinguifhed this conclu-ding Year; and thefe therefore I think it my duty to lay before Them.

The firft article, which I fhall fpecify, becaufe it is an article of fingular Honour to my Work, is this — that *the Subfcription*, fo far from finking to-wards the clofe of this long Work, was in the year 1768 larger than at any time before, and in *this* the concluding year it has rifen above the year preceding.

The Augmentation, in this laft year, is princi-pally owing to the Munificence of *His Moft Serene Highnefs*, The Prince of Orange, *Stadtholder, Captain General &c. of The United Provinces*; the great Honour of whofe Patronage is here acknow-ledged with the utmoft gratitude. The addition of this exalted Name, a Name juftly dear to every true Englifhman, gives the chief Luftre to this Undertaking — next to The Auguft Name of The Sovereign of thefe Kingdoms, His Britannic Majesty. The Patronage of His Moft Serene Highnefs, unfollicited from hence, was benevo-lently obtained by the application of that Mæcenas of Literature *Greffier* Fagel; and to Him the State of this Work had been made known by the learned and very celebrated Mr *Chais* at the Hague.

This reverend and worthy Gentleman (who has obliged the World with an excellent Illuftration of the Old Teftament, as far as the end of *Samuel*) furprized me by the notice of this Patronage ; in a Letter fo exceedingly obliging, and fo very honourable both to my Work and to myfelf, that I cannot deny my Friends the pleafure of perufing it.

Monfieur

Quoique je n'aie pas l'honneur d'etre connu de Vous je n'ai pas laiffé de prendre une part fincére au louable deffein, dont l'exécution Vous occupe, et à la gloire dont Vous Vous couvrez par la conftance de vos efforts, pour rendre autant qu'il fera poffible au Texte Sacre du V. T. fa pureté originale ; en collationnant une multitude de Manufcripts Hebreux, jufqu'ici négligés, ou inconnus.

L'expofition que Vous avez faite Vous meme de votre projet, le compte que Vous avez rendu annuellement de vos premieres découvertes, et plus encore vos favantes Differtations, ont fuffifamment inftruit le Public, de ce que l'Eglife peut attendre, de votre zele, de votre habileté, et de votre patience, dans la conduite d'une entreprife, dont le but fait l'éloge, et dont le fuccès intereffe fi directement l'honneur de la Religion et de fes Miniftres.

Votre dernier écrit en particulier (je parle, Monfieur, de vos doctes Obfervations fur le célébre paffage du 1. Livre de Samuel Chap. VI. 19) a achevé de rendre la chofe fenfible, aux perfonnes memes, en qui l'amour de la vérité n'eft accompagné d'aucun des fecours

de

de l'érudition. Et si, pour donner un nouveau relief à vos travaux, aux yeux des Savans, que leur goût ou leur vocation attachent à l'étude de la littérature orientale, il ne falloit plus, que munir vos recherches, du Sceau d'une approbation généralement respectée, qu'est ce qu'on peut y desirer, après l'approbation distinguée du Prelat illustre, à qui le Public est redevable de l'incomparable Traité sur la Poesie des Hebreux?

J'aurois cru, Monsieur, qu'après le suffrage d'un si grand Juge, sans compter les applaudissemens, de tant d'autres Savans dont les Royaumes Britanniques abbondent, et l'accueil unanime que ceux des pays d'en deça la mer ont fait à vos demarches et à vos productions, tout auroit concouru à applanir sous vos pas les difficultés qui retardent l'entier accomplissement d'un Ouvrage, dont l'importance est si universellement reconnue. Ce n'a été qu'avec une surprise extreme, que j'ai vu par votre Lettre à Milord Eveque d'Oxford, que les secours manquent encore à vos voeux; et cela meme, Monsieur, m'a fait presumer, qu'assurément votre modestie desservoit votre zèle, contre vos propres desirs.

J'ai une preuve à Vous en donner, qui ne sauroit Vous déplaire. Tout récemment une Personne, que son rang et sa pieté rendent doublement respectable, a bien voulu se prêter à entretenir Monseigneur le Prince d'Orange, de l'utilité de vos Travaux, et du point où Vous avez deja amené le grand Ouvrage, dont Vous Vous êtes chargé. Ce Prince, digne héritier des Vertus de ses glorieux Ancêtres, aime la Religion parce qu'il la connoit. On le trouve toujours pret à se porter avec

ardeur,

ardeur, à tout ce qui peut en etendre l'empire, par des moyens dignes d'elle, par ce qu'il en sent l'excellence et qu'une pieté éclairée anime en lui un penchant genereux à procurer le bonheur du genre humain. Dès qu'il a été bien instruit de vos vûes et de leur importance, il a temoigné, qu'il se feroit un plaisir d'en encourager l'exécution. Tout de suite, il y a destiné Cinquante Livres Sterling par an, pour le temps convenable; si je ne me trompe pour cinq ans: et j'ai ordre, Monsieur, de Vous le faire savoir, afin que Vous puissiez prendre des mesures, pour jouir dès que Vous le trouverez à propos, des commencemens d'une faveur, qui sans doute Vous paroitra d'autant plus précieuse, que Vous ne Vous y attendiez pas.

Si mes soins peuvent Vous être de quelque utilité soit pour faire parvenir vos sentimens à Monseigneur le Prince Stadhouder, soit pour recevoir du Thrésorier de S. A. S. la somme qui Vous est actuellement assignée; Vous n'avez, Monsieur, qu' à disposer de moi. C'est avec les sentimens d'une considération distinguée, et au milieu des voeux les plus purs, pour vôtre conservation et pour le succès de vos pieux travaux, que j'ai l'honneur d'etre,

Monsieur,   Votre très humble

& très obeïssant Serviteur

A la Haye,
le 22 Mars 1769.

C. CHAIS

Pasteur Emérite de l'Eglise
Walonne de la Haye.

The *Eight* MSS, belonging to His Majesty THE KING OF DENMARK, which had been collated for me at *Copenhagen*, have been in this year sent to England, and brought to Oxford, for my own personal inspection of them: as I was particularly desirous of seeing the *Characters*, and *Modes of Writing*, together with *the Ages*, of those MSS, which had been, with a Liberality so truly Royal, collected out of *Africa* and *Asia*. And I beg leave, in this public manner likewise, to express my warmest Thanks to The Royal Proprietor of these valuable MSS; for having, in a very condescending manner, both promised them, and caused them to be sent hither. The time, when I applied for a sight of these MSS, was soon after His Danish Majesty had honoured our University with His Presence; and with His gracious Acceptance of that profound Respect, which we were proud of shewing to so Amiable a Monarch. And as this signal Favour, of commanding all these MSS to be sent hither, was in a great measure granted by way of *Compliment to this University*; it is necessary, that such a Compliment should be ascertained. The following is therefore the Letter, with which I was then honoured, and I acknowledge myself honoured exceedingly, by my Illustrious Friend His Excellency *The Count* DE BERNSTORFF.

Rev.

Rev^d. Sir,

I acknowledge most gratefully your kind Remembrance, and the Proofs of the same with which You have been pleased to honour me in your much esteem'd Letter of the 21st. instant. I beg You will be fully persuaded, Rev^d. Sir, of my constant and ardent Desire to shew You upon every occasion, how great a Value I put upon your Friendship, how glad I am to have had the Pleasure of making your personal Acquaintance, and how sincerely I wish to do You any Service in my Power. It is in consequence a real Satisfaction to me to be able to inform You, Rev^d. Sir, that your Desires having been laid before the King, His Majesty, out of a true Regard for the University of Oxford, and particularly in order to assist You in your laudable Undertaking, has been pleased to grant your Request without any difficulty. I am sorry to see the Season of the Year so far advanced, and the Risks of the Sea in the approaching Winter-Months so considerable, that the immediate Conveyance of the MSS from Copenhagen to Baron Diede will not be thought safe under these circumstances. But I shall not be wanting, in obedience to His Majesty's Orders, to take due Care, after my return to Denmark, to see them transmitted hither, for your Use and Examination, by the very first Opportunity. I beg, You will depend upon it, Rev^d. Sir; and be assured of the sentiments of great Truth and distinguish'd Esteem, with which I have the Honour to be, Rev^d. Sir,

Your most obedient humble Servant,

London,
Sept. 29, 1768. BERNSTORFF.

Another article, in the courfe of this year, highly honourable to this Work, is — that one MS, belonging to the Archiepifcopal library of *St Sepulchre* in *Dublin*, has been obligingly collated for me by my Friend The Right Reverend *The Lord Bifhop of* DROMORE; affifted by the learned and worthy Dr *Forfayeth*, Hebrew Profeffor in Trinity College, Dublin. And a greater Honour could not have been done to any part of the Work, than to have it performed by a Prelate of fuch diftinguifhed Abilities in general; and whofe uncommon Knowledge of the Original Languages of the Bible is well known to thofe, who are happy in His Lordfhip's Acquaintance.

The next article, which demands my prefent Thanks, is the Favour fhewn to my Work by the learned Profeffor *Lilienthal*, Head-Librarian at *Koenigfberg*; where, in the Royal library, are 2 Hebrew MSS. Thefe has the worthy Profeffor been fo good as to collate, unfollicited by me, and unrewarded — excepting by my grateful Acknowledgment of the Services he has done to the Public, by promoting the perfection of this Work. In the very accurate Collations, which I have received of thefe MSS, are found many and valuable Various Readings: the firft MS contains the *Pentateuch*, *Megilloth*, *Haphtaroth*, *Job*, and part of *Jeremiah*; the fecond contains the *Prophets* and *Hagiographa*.

U 2

In

In the Accounts for 1767 and 1768 (fee pages 116 and 128) mention was made of Profeffor *Nagel*, at *Altdorff*; and of his being generoufly employed to collate, for this Work, 4 Hebrew MSS, preferved at *Nuremberg*: the firft of which is a magnificent MS, in 7 Folio volumes, containing the whole Hebrew Bible. The collations of thefe MSS, fo far as they contain from the beginning of *Genefis* to the end of *Kings*, have been tranfmitted to me, and received, in the prefent year; together with many Variations, out of the *Talmuds* both of *Jerufalem* and *Babylon*, and out of other books of Rabbinical Antiquity. And for this very acceptable Prefent, though but a part of the intended Benefaction, I here exprefs my beft Thanks to the Illuftrious Perfons, who have ordered the Collations to be made, and to the learned Profeffor for his Care in making them. The remainder of that Collection, when finifhed, will be received with equal thankfulnefs.

But here, a doubt may arife with fome of my Readers; who may not readily reconcile what was faid before, concerning *this Work being now concluded*, with what is faid in the laft paragraph, concerning *further addition to be ftill made to it*. And this circumftance leads me to enlarge here, on what will conftitute a very material part of the prefent Account; namely, an Anfwer to this Queftion — *What is to be now done with this Collation of the Hebrew MSS?* And, in order to the forming of an

Anfwer properly, it is neceffary to confider —— *What this Collation was to be* — and *What it is.*

Let it then be recollected here, that the Work engaged for was — to collate all the MSS of the Hebrew Bible, in our own Country ; and, during the progrefs of fuch Collation at home, to procure the Various Readings of fome of the beft MSS abroad.

Now the number of Hebrew MSS, preferved in *our own* Kingdoms, which have been collated on this occafion, amounts to 140. The number of *Foreign* Collations, received already, and likely to be received foon, amounts to 113. And the Collations of the whole, or parts, of the *printed* Hebrew Bible, are 12. Confequently, the Total of Collations, for the benefit of this Work, is 265 : probably more, by above 100, than have as yet been made of any other antient Book, even of the *New Teftament* — though the *Old* Teftament is nearly three times larger than the *New* ; the Verfes in the former being 23185, and in the latter being only 7959. And it will not perhaps be forgotten, that notwithftanding this great difference in the fize of thefe volumes of the *Old* and *New* Teftament, and the ftill greater difference in collating the *Greek* MSS by *whole Words*, and the *Hebrew* MSS by *fingle Letters* ; yet did the New Teftament employ the very learned and very laborious Dr *Mill* (here at OXFORD likewife) not *Ten* years only, but *Thirty.*

But,

But, though the Collation, thus undertaken, be now finished; there must be an interval *of some Years*, before this Work can be prepared for the Prefs; and of *some more Years*, before it can be published. During the last of these periods, it will not be easy to insert regularly any new Collations; but during the first period, and especially in the earlier parts of it, it will be very practicable to add, and regularly to insert, all such Collations as may hereafter arrive from abroad.

If therefore it shall be thought adviseable, (as I have not the least doubt but it will) that this Work should be prepared for the Prefs; that is, that all the Various Readings, now contained in TWO HUNDRED AND SIXTY FIVE distinct and separate Parcels, should be selected, sorted, connected regularly, and disposed uniformly, in the most concise yet most intelligible and clear method, at one view, under the proper Verse of every Chapter through the Old Testament: while this extensive Operation shall be preparing and carrying on, there will be opportunity for inserting the Various Readings of other *Foreign* Collations, especially all such as may arrive within the next Two Years.

The first among the Collations not yet received, but the soonest expected, are those placed foremost in the following Catalogue.

1. Collations

1. Collations of 2 MSS, in the public library at STRASBURG, are every day expected; and these are to be followed by Collations of 7 other MSS in the same library: all which are very generously presented to me, for this Work, by the learned and worthy Librarian Mr *Oberlin*.

2. This Work will be further enriched soon by the kindness of the learned Mr *Schnurrer* of Wirtemberg; who has obligingly acquainted me with his having collated for me a valuable MS in the public library at JENA.

3. The Remainder of the Collations of the 4 MSS &c: at NUREMBERG, now carrying on by Professor *Nagel*.

4. My learned Friend Monf. L'Abbé *Affeline*, Professor at the *Sorbonne*, having most obligingly offered me his assistance, in some further Collations at PARIS; I have no doubt, but I shall be soon favoured with some fresh proofs of his benevolence to my Work and me.

5. The MS at BRIEG in Silesia, which has been said to contain very many Variations, has been collated at my request. This Collation has been kindly forwarded to Berlin, by the Reverend Mr *Loos*, Chaplain to His Majesty THE KING OF PRUSSIA; and it has been lately sent from Berlin to London.

6. The

6. The Collation of the oldeſt and beſt of the Hebrew MSS, in the Royal Library at B E R L I N, is, I make no doubt, nearly completed: and I expect as much Satisfaction from the laſt part, as I have received from the former parts, already ſent me by the Collator, the learned Profeſſor *Murſinna.*

7. A Collation of a MS of the whole Hebrew Bible at C O L O G N E having been agreed on, for ſome years ſince, in conſequence of Letters with which I was honoured by the learned Dr *Hilleſheim,* Rector of the Univerſity in that city; there is great reaſon to expect the ſpeedy arrival of its Various Readings.

8. The oldeſt and beſt of the MSS at E R F U R T, which were beforementioned, has been for ſome time under the examination of the learned Profeſſor and Librarian Mr *Bahrdt*; in conſequence of whoſe care and fidelity, I make no doubt of recei-ving a very valuable Collation of that MS. The laſt Letter, with which he favoured me, not only gave me reaſon to expect, that this Collation will be ſoon in England; but alſo promiſed me, in a very obliging manner, ſome Various Readings from 3 MSS at L E I P S I C and from 1 at D R E S D E N.

9. At M I L A N there ſtill remains to be collated the MS of the *Samaritan* Pentateuch, which Mont-faucon has recommended, as very worthy of exa-mination.

mination. And I have no doubt of receiving soon a good Collation of it, from the learned Professor *Henrico A Porta*, or the learned Librarian Dr *Baptista Branca*; who have now collated for me all the Hebrew MSS in the *Ambrosian* library.

10. In the public library at L E Y D E N is preserved another MS of the *Samaritan* Pentateuch; of which I am still in hopes of receiving a Collation, through the favour of the learned Professor *Schultens*, who has kindly entertained thoughts of it: and, if not from himself, yet from some other person selected by him, and acting under his direction. See page 58.

11. But, as my wishes have extended themselves to every Quarter of the World; and as my hopes have been more than answered by the MSS in E u r o p e and from A f r i c a : so I now congratulate the Public, on the information lately sent me by the Reverend Dr *Cooper*, President of King's College, New York, in A m e r i c a. This information is, that *Mr Sampson Simson, a very worthy and benevolent old Gentleman, of the Jewish persuasion, living in that city, is in possession of a MS of very great antiquity, containing the whole Hebrew Bible; which he probably would send to England for my use, if I properly requested it.* This I have done accordingly; and I do here express my thanks as heartily to the *President* for his notice, as I shall to the *Possessor* of the MS, if he obligingly favours me with the sight of it.

W   12. In

12. In ASIA likewise have been made several enquiries after Hebrew MSS ; in the countries near *Madrafs*, by the late Governor *Robert Palke* Efq; a liberal Patron of this Work ; and in the countries near *Aleppo*, by the late Mr *Dawes*, Chaplain there to the Britifh Factory. And as there was, even fo late as about 30 years ago, preferved at *Naploufe* (antiently *Sichem*, near mount Gerizim) a very old MS of the *Samaritan Pentateuch*, belonging to the fmall remnant of the *Samaritans* in that place ; I fome time fince earneftly entreated two Friends to try, whether the poffeffors of this MS might not be prevailed on, by a handfome Sum of Money, to accept a printed copy, in exchange for it.

Laftly : that nothing might be left unattempted, where fuccefs was but barely poffible, I fome time fince, by means of the reverend and very learned Dr *Jubb*, folicited his friend *Frederick Pigou*, Efq; (a Gentleman, as perfectly able, as he was found perfectly willing) to make the beft enquiry after Hebrew MSS in CHINA. By this Gentleman's benevolent affiftance, I fent a Commiffion, for purchafing (if poffible) fuch a MS from the Jews in the province of *Ho-nan:* or elfe, to reward fome perfon for collating at leaft part of their written Pentateuch with our printed copy ; in order to which I fent, at the fame time, *Van der Hooght*'s edition. And notice is juft arrived from *China*, that

that this enquiry is in a fair train ; a Friend at *Canton* having promised to procure, if poffible, a MS from thofe Jews in *Ho-nan*, by the affiftance of the Bifhop of that Province.

Thus have I attempted to lay before the Reader a hiftory of my Collation ; and of my endeavours to execute the great Truft repofed in me by the Patrons of my Undertaking. *What the Collation was to be*, has been fet forth ; and *What it is*, has been fet forth likewife. But whether, in the profecution of it, during the paft Ten Years, I have, or have not, attended to it with all the Care poffible — can be certain only to thofe, who know that my general rule has been, to devote to it 10 or 12 hours in a day, and frequently 14 ; at leaft, that this *was* my practice, till fuch fevere application became no longer poffible, through the Injuries done to my Conftitution.

But here it may be faid — that, even admitting the truth of the preceding paragraph, yet, as the Care taken by *any one* perfon, how great foever, is but the Care taken by *One* ; how can that One anfwer for the Carefulnefs of *Others :* of thofe, whom he has employed as his Affiftants, and whofe parts of the Work he cannot have entirely re-examined ? My anfwer is this. The Patrons of this Work are too prudent, to have expected what was plainly impoffible. A Work, which cannot be done by *one* man, muft, if done at all, be done by *more*

than

than one. And that Collation, which could not be *made* by one man, could not be *revised* by one; becaufe entirely to revife the whole is to examine each Collation, as to *every thing* either *noted* or *omitted*: which certainly amounts to a Recollation.

All therefore, which could reafonably be expected, was — that the Conductor of the Work, thus neceffarily affifted by others, fhould felect the fitteft and moft careful among fuch as would fubmit to the Employment; and direct, fuperintend, and in many particulars revife their feveral labours, as far as was practicable. No perfons have been employed to collate MSS, who were not properly inftructed, and well qualified to defcribe all the *common* Variations: and the fixed rule has been, that every Variation, which was uncommon and difficult, was marked for *my own* examination. In general; before a perfon was admitted to collate any MS, he was firft of all exercifed in *tranfcribing* Collations before made; then was tried in *collating* part of a MS well *collated before*: and, when thus proved to be careful and exact, has been then entrufted with an uncollated MS, under the reftriction fpecified in the preceding fentence. And, after all, that every degree of fatisfaction may be given, which can be given, to *my own* mind as well as to the minds of others; it is my fixed intention (if I live, and am fufficiently encouraged to prepare this Work for the Prefs) to re-examine, with my own eyes, all the MSS in England, in many of the
moft

moſt important paſſages : that ſo this Work may appear with *as much Perfection*, as my care can give to it.

The word *Perfection* is here limited, becauſe I am ſenſible of my own fallibility; and becauſe the proſecution of this Work has furniſhed out numerous proofs — how very eaſy it is to err, or rather, how impoſſible it is not to err ſometimes, in reading and writing Letters, which are ſo exceedingly ſimilar to each other. So that, among all the Works ever ſet on foot in the world, this is *that*, which has the ſtrongeſt apology to offer, I will not ſay for *the few*, but for *the many*, Miſtakes ;

———— *quas aut incuria fudit,*
Aut humana parum cavit natura ————

As to the *general perfection* of this Work, it may be objected — that it cannot with any propriety claim that title ; becauſe there remain ſo many other MSS, in Europe, at preſent uncollated. This is very readily acknowledged. However, I would aſk — Whether the *New* Teſtament by Dr *Mill* was not received with very high and juſt Applauſe by the Learned ; when yet, that illuſtrious Work was only *ſo far perfect*, as to contain (perhaps regular and entire) Collations of about 112 MSS ? †
And when, after the additional Collations made by *Kuſter, Bengelius, Wetſtein* &c : there are ſtill

† The *Veleſian* and *Wechelian* Variations are here excepted ; becauſe I have ſeen no ſatisfactory account of them.

at leaft 100 *MSS*, containing *the whole or parts of the New Teftament, the Various Readings of which have not yet been collected at all ; at leaft, have never yet been made public.* What then would the World have faid, ftill more juftly, in praife of Dr *Mill's* Edition ; had he been previoufly enabled, either in perfon, or by fome other Man of learning felected for that Commiffion, to examine *almoft all the uncollated* Greek MSS, in at leaft *fome hundreds of the moft important paffages ?*

Now that, which would have derived fo much additional dignity, and given a *Perfection* much more properly fo called, to that Oxford edition of the *New* Teftament, that very Plan (and let not my Patrons be furprifed, if I venture to attempt every thing for *Their* greater Honour) that very Plan I have prepared to carry into execution, as to this Oxford edition of the *Old* Teftament.

By way of trial, how far Improvements might be derived to my Work ; if fuch of the Foreign MSS, as were not collated, fhould be examined only in particular paffages : in the year 1767, I made a vifit to the Hebrew MSS in P a r i s. And I found, that even a partial examination, when limited to the paffages of greater importance, would be attended with very happy confequences ; as it would, if extended *through Europe*, enrich the Work with the Variations of *almoft all the known MSS*, in fuch paffages of the Old Teftament as

are

are of particular moment; and especially in those, which, though quoted in the *New* Testament, do not now perfectly agree with such Quotations.

The further prosecution of this Plan, thus recommended by my own personal experience, is now to be carried into execution, through *Europe*: not indeed by myself, whom I consider as reserved for the continuance of Labour at home; but by Mr PAUL JACOB BRUNS, of *Lubec* — on whose Fitness for such a Commission, in point of *Ability* and of *Fidelity*, I think the Patrons of this Work may securely depend. This learned Gentleman has been frequently mentioned in the preceding Accounts (see pages 97, 102, 113, 116, 121) as having collated for me at *Carlsruhe*, and as having come to me and assisted me at *Paris*. And, after many proofs of his Zeal for this Work *abroad*; he has been for several Months, and is still, with me at *Oxford*: in order to furnish himself, as perfectly as possible, with the various particulars of his future Enquiries.

Thus have I endeavoured, and I hope not without success, to give that Satisfaction to my PATRONS, which They have the utmost Right to expect; as to the *Commencement*, the *Conduct*, and the *Conclusion*, of my Collation.

With regard to the Preparation of this Work for the Press; as some may be desirous of knowing,

ing, how many Years that Preparation will require: all that I can fay at prefent is, that I am certain only of thefe two things — Firft; that (when the difficulty of fixing upon *The moft proper Method* fhall have been got over) the felecting, connecting, adapting, tranfcribing, and re-tranfcribing fuch an infinity of Materials, will (if poffible) exceed in fatigue even the paft Collation — Secondly; that, if I fhould fix a period (which indeed is not in my power) even *that* would fubject me to as rigid a Slavery, as I have already experienced from fixing a former Term: and this, at an advanced Time of Life, and under a broken State of Health; both which require much more Exercife, and lefs intenfive Application, than I have for the laft Twenty Years allowed myfelf.

But, as my P A T R O N S may in fome meafure judge, from the preceding State of things, what Expence ftill attends my Work abroad, in the way of Collation; and what Expence may be neceffary for the purchafe of fome MSS in *Afia*, where they cannot be collated: fince they fee alfo the voluntary but expenfive Engagement I have entered into, for the further Examination of the *European* MSS; and fince they will certainly conclude, that this Work cannot be prepared by me for the Prefs, without feveral Affiftants: it muft be, and is here, humbly fubmitted to The Greater and More Illuftrious among my P A T R O N S, upon what Plan of *Support* and *Encouragement* I am now to proceed.

The paſt Subſcription was formed ; in order to enable me to diſcharge the vaſt Expence of the Collation, as at firſt undertaken ; and it has more than anſwered its original purpoſe, becauſe it has enabled me to make that Work more complete, by procuring the examinations of more MSS, than I at firſt thought poſſible.

I do not ſuppoſe, that any perſons can be found, who will declare it as their ſober opinion — that *I ought to be condemned to hard Labour for the reſt of my Life*, merely, *as a Reward for paſt Services*. But I do know, that there are men ; who, from a conviction that T H E Y would have made Such a Subſcription very lucrative to *Themſelves*, have been mighty ready to intimate — that, no doubt, the Collator of the Hebrew MSS has done the ſame. And, as I have not forgot the promiſe, which I made in page 139 ; I ſhall here proceed to ſatisfy ſome perſons, and to ſilence others, by the following explicit declarations.

The ſeveral Subſcriptions, which have appeared in the Annual Accounts for the paſt Nine Years, when reduced by ſome articles not paid at all, and enlarged by other articles paid afterwards, have (upon the moſt exact computation which I can make) amounted in each Year to the Total Sums here following.

Year 1, being 1760 ———	£ 506	7	0
—— 2 —— 1761 ———	910	7	6
—— 3 —— 1762 ———	902	15	6
—— 4 —— 1763 ———	979	8	6
—— 5 —— 1764 ———	958	8	0
—— 6 —— 1765 ———	937	8	0
—— 7 —— 1766 ———	961	11	0
—— 8 —— 1767 ———	976	5	0
—— 9 —— 1768 ———	980	11	0
	8113	1	6

In this Tenth and concluding Year, 1769, my Work has been honoured with the following additional Benefactors.

His Moſt Serene Highneſs . The PRINCE of ORANGE }	£ 50	0	0
Anonymous	20	0	0
John Delmé, Eſq;	10	10	0
Rev. Dr Domvile . . . . ˙ .	3	3	0
Freeman Flower, Eſq;	2	2	0
Sir Henry Hoghton, Bart . . .	5	5	0
Henry Hunt, Eſq; Tipperary . .	1	1	0
Rev. Mr Joſeph Jane	2	2	0
Rev. Dr Markham, Whitechapel .	1	1	0
Robert Palke, Eſq;	5	5	0
Rev. Dr John Scrope	1	1	0
	101	10	0

Which Sum, added to } —— already received }	.	660	6	0
and to what *probably* will } be received farther . }	.	242	10	0
amounts to .	1004	6	0

Nine Years	8113	1	6
Tenth Year	1004	6	0
TOTAL £	9117	7	6

Reader! What a Sum is here! Let Foreign Nations read, with aftonifhment, this ftory of *Britons* and *Their* KING ; joined by One Foreign *Prince* and One Foreign *Academy:* voluntarily contributing, for Ten Years, their feveral Bounties, with a degree of Public Spirit beyond all Example, for the Accomplifhment of a Work purely fubfervient to *The Honour of Revelation* ; a Work, facred to *The Glory of* GOD and *The Good of* MANKIND! And under the powerful influence of *this* view of my Work, it is impoffible for me to be fufficiently thankful —— either to THOSE, who have honoured with their Patronage *me*, as the humble Inftrument in beginning and compleating it — or to DIVINE PROVIDENCE, for granting me Life to finifh it, as well as Refolution to undertake it.

X 2   But

But — I hear the Whisper of Detraction ; representing all this, as an empty parade of words : and intimating what a comfortable thing a Truft of *Nine Thoufand Pounds* muft be, in the hands of any man, who had in a great meafure the fecret Difpofal of it. Intimations of this nature are not new ; they have long attended the profperous State of my Subfcription. But His late Grace of Canterbury, and fome other of my Principal Patrons, after perufing (about three years fince) fome account of the Subfcription, of the Expence attending the Work, and of the Emolument of it to myfelf, agreed in expreffing their higheft Satisfaction ; and indeed wondered at the *Difintereftednefs*, with which I had managed fo ample a Subfcription.

I do not mean, however, to offer merely an appeal to His Grace, now dead ; or to fome of the Higheft Perfons in the Church, now living, who knew His Grace's fentiments, and honoured me with their own, upon that occafion. I would willingly declare to every Subfcriber every thing he would be glad to know, as to every part of my conduct, in this great Affair — fo far, I mean, as is poffible. But, a particular detail of all the various articles of Expence, in fo very involved and fo very perplexing a Tranfaction, cannot be expected ; and, if expected, cannot be granted to others, becaufe I have it not myfelf. And yet, that this may not be conftrued into a fubterfuge ;

I will

I will do, what perhaps few of my Subscribers look for, and what most of Them will be surprised and concerned at. I will now endeavour to furnish out some general notion, concerning my Management; which notion, though general, will perhaps enable every Reader to estimate — *What a great Fortune I have made from my Subscription!*

There is one point, in which all men will agree at once; and it is this — that *I ought, at least, to have lived upon my Subscription.*

From this single and simple principle, supposed to be universally granted, it follows — that *I ought to have laid by, unspent, whatever Income I had, exclusive of this Subscription.*

But the other articles of my Income, during these Ten Years, added to some Money (clear of Debt) antecedent to this Undertaking, amount to the whole Sum I am now possessed of — excepting about 500 £.

Consequently; instead of near 5000 £ — which, in the opinion of some of my Chief Patrons, ought to have been reserved to myself — and which, if I had meant to be my own Pay-Master, and not consulted the Honour of my Work, I might have secured — I find myself possessed of about 500 £ in virtue of This Subscription: after *Ten Years* spent in recommending such a Work to others, and another *Ten Years* spent by myself in the execution of it.

The

The Reader will probably be furprifed, at finding that 500 l. is the utmoft I poffefs, as arifing out of this Subfcription. And perhaps he will be furprifed, ftill more, at the following notices — that in this Sum is included the whole confequence of this Year's Subfcription, and therefore of the whole Subfcription — but, that even this Sum, fo referved, is only referved *at prefent*, and by no means referved for *myfelf*; becaufe it is already devoted to the further Expences of my Work : and the further Expences, already engaged for, are thefe.

1. For the Collations of 4 MSS, and a large part of a 5th, not yet received, nor paid for ; the firft, at *Brieg*, in Silefia ; the fecond, at *Cologne* ; the third, at *Erfurt* ; the fourth, at *Milan* ; and the fifth, at *Berlin*.   See pages 159 and 160.

2. Poffibly, for purchafing MSS in *Afia* ; at *Naploufe* and *Ho - nan*.   See page 162.

3. Probably, for employing perfons, to collate the MS, which may reafonably be expected from *America*.   See page 161.

4. Certainly, for employing perfons, to tranfcribe the remainder of the feveral Collations made lately.

5. And laftly, for the Examinations to be made of MSS, throughout Europe ; which may take up near *Two Years* time.

Now

Now if this 5th and laſt particular ſhall, as per-haps it will, require the Sum of 500 *l*; if this one article only ſhall require this ſmall remainder of the Subſcription : *how are to be diſcharged* the Expences of the other 4 articles ? It is not impoſſible, but ſome of my Readers may demand an Anſwer; and perhaps expect me to ſay, Whether I will diſcover my own folly, ſtill further, by laying out upon my Work *part of my private Income*, as well as the Subſcription ? The reply is, that *I cannot now help it* : and indeed, even the Sum of 200 £, which may be neceſſary for the 4 other articles of Expence before ſpecified, is *by no means the largeſt Donation, made to my Work, out of my private Income.*

But, I will ſpecify no further; at leaſt, thus publickly. Nor would I have inſerted here the moſt diſtant alluſion to the preceding circumſtan-ces; had not the *ſuppoſed Gain* from my Work been ſo very often, and ſo very ſtudiouſly, magni-fied. And a man muſt have much leſs Spirit, than the conductor of this Work has ſtill left ; who would not ſignify his Contempt of ſuch Miſrepre-ſentation, at the time when it was become his in-diſpenſable duty to undeceive his Principal Patrons. In ſhort: as to the ſum of 200 £, juſt before mentioned ; the diſcharge of that Ex-pence will be the more eaſy to me, on account of the Legacy of 200 £, mentioned in page 123. This Legacy, the Executor has obligingly aſſured me me, fhall be paid, as devifed ; that is, *upon my finifhing the Collation, which I had undertaken.* And from this circumftance it appears, that the idea of the L A D Y, my P A T R O N E S S, in this generous Bequeft, was not — Her affifting to defray the Expence of my Work, but — Her contributing to the Reward for completing it.

I fhall now conclude this long Account of the Work, and of my own Conduct in it, with the Name of every Perfon (whom I am at liberty to name) that has at all fubfcribed towards it. And I fhall only add — that, whenever this Collation fhall be publifhed, for the *common Advantage of all Europe* ; and when, in confequence of this Collation, there fhall be, for *our own* particular Benefit, *a Revifal of our Englifh Tranflation* ; when The Holy Scripture fhall be hereby rendered more intelligible and more inftructive to thofe, who believe its Divine Authority, as well as more confiftent and more convincing to thofe, who doubt or difbelieve : then will every juft Encomium be gratefully beftowed on

THE ROYAL,

The I L L U S T R I O U S, and The L E A R N E D,

who have patronized this Work ; and whofe Names will not only be prefixed to this Work hereafter, but alfo are at prefent collected together, and adorn the following C A T A L O G U E.

PATRONS.

THE

KING.

His Moſt Serene Highneſs
The PRINCE of ORANGE.

The UNIVERSITIES of
OXFORD, CAMBRIDGE,
DUBLIN.
.

The *Theodore-Palatine* Academy at
MANNHEIM.

Affleck, Rev. Mr

Aguilar, Honourable Baron

Allen (late) Ralph, Efq;

All Souls College

Amyatt, James, Efq;

Andrew, Rev. Dr, Preb. Rochefter

Afhton, Rev. Dr, Fell. Eton College

Atherton, Rev. Mr

Atwell (late) Rev. Dr, Preb. Gloucefter

Avery (late) Dr Benjamin

Aylmer, Hon. and Rev. Mr, Preb. Briftol

Barford, Rev. Mr

Barker, Thomas, Efq;

Barnard, Rev. Dr, Provoft Eton College

Barrington, Hon. and Rt Rev. Lord Bp Landaff

Bafket, Thomas, Efq;

Bate, Rev. Mr Chambers

Bate, Rev. Mr James, Deptford

Bath (late) Right Honourable, Earl

Bearcroft (late) Rev. Dr

Bell, Rev. Dr, Preb. Weftminfter

Benfon (late) Rev. Dr

Bentham, Rev. Dr, Reg. Prof. Divinity, Oxford

Blacket, Rev. Dr

Blackftone, William, Efq;

Bland

Bland (late) Rev. Dr, Preb. Durham
Bolton (late) Rev. Dr, Dean Carlisle
Bouchery, Rev. Mr
Brasen - Nose College
Bristol, Dean and Chapter
Bryant, Jacob, Esq;
Burrow, James, Esq;
Burton, Rev. Dr Daniel, Chancellor Oxford
Burton (late) Rev. Dr Thomas, Preb. Durham
Bute, Right Honourable, Earl
Butler, Rev. Dr

Campbell, John, Esq;
Canterbury, Dean and Chapter
Chamberlayne, Rev. Mr
Chambers, Rev. Dr
Chandler (late) Rev. Dr Samuel
Channing, Mr John
Chapman, Rev. Dr John
Chenevix, Right Rev. Lord Bishop Waterford
Cholwich, Rev. Dr, Preb. Exeter
Clark, Mr William
Collet, Dr
Conant, Rev. Mr
Cornwallis, His Grace, Lord Arch-Bp Canterbury
Corpus - Christi College

Cowper,

Cowper, Hon. and Rev. Dr, Dean Durham
Cox, His Grace, Lord Arch-Bishop Cashell
Cracherode, Rev. Mr
Craufurd (late) Honourable General
Cuſt, Right Honourable Sir John, Speaker H. C.
Cuſt, Rev. Dr, Canon Chriſt-Church
Cuſt, Peregrine, Eſq;

Da Coſta (late) Solomon, Eſq;
Daddo (late) Rev. Mr
Damer, Honourable John, Eſq;
Delmé, Peter, Eſq;
Delmé, John, Eſq;
Devonſhire (late) His Grace, Duke
Dickens, Rev. Archdeacon, D. D.
Dodſon, Michael, Eſq;
Domville, Rev. Dr, Dublin
Douglas, Rev. Dr James, Preb. Durham
Douglas, Rev. Dr John, Can. Windſor
Drummond, His Grace, Lord Arch-Bishop York
Duane, Matthew, Eſq;
Durell, Rev. Dr, Principal Hertford College
Durell (late) Rev. Mr
Durham, Dean and Chapter

Edwards,

Edwards, Rev. Dr, Coventry
Egerton, Right Rev. Ld Bp Litchfield & Coventry
Ellis (late) Right Rev. Lord Bishop St David's
Eton College
Exeter, Right Honourable, Earl
Exeter, Dean and Chapter
Exeter College
Eyre, Rev. Dr

Fanshaw (late) Rev. Dr, Reg. Prof. Div. Oxford
Farmer, Rev. Mr
Flower, Freeman, Esq;
Fordyce, Rev. Dr
Fothergill, Rev. Dr, Provost Queen's College
Freind (late) Rev. Dr, Dean Canterbury
Fuller, Richard, Esq;
Furneaux, Rev. Dr

Gabriel, Rev. Dr
Gadsden, Chr. Esq; Charles-Town, South Carolina
Garnet, Right Rev. Lord Bishop Clogher
Gawsell (late) Rev. Mr
Geach, Mr Francis
Gibbons, Rev. Dr
Gifford, Rev. Dr
Gilbert (late) His Grace, Lord Arch-Bp York

Gill,

Gill, Rev. Dr
Gloucester, Dean and Chapter
Golding (late) Rev. Dr, Warden Winchester
Gould, Rev. Mr, Clare - Hall
Granville (late) Right Honourable, Earl
Gray, Charles, Esq;
Green, Right Rev. Lord Bishop Lincoln
Greet, Rev. Mr
Gregory (late) Rev. Dr, Dean Christ-Church
Grenville, Right Honourable George

Hallifax, Right Honourable Earl
Hanbury (late) William, Esq;
Hardwicke (late) Right Honourable Earl
Hardwicke, Right Honourable Earl
Harris, Rev. Mr
Hawkins, John, Esq;
Hayter (late) Right Rev. Lord Bishop London
Heberden, Dr William
Henley (late) Rev. Mr
Hesse, John Adam Frederick, Esq;
Hetherington, Rev. Mr, Fellow Eton
Hill, Rev. Dr, Treasurer Armagh
Hoadly (late) Right Rev. Lord Bishop Winchester
Hoadly, Rev. Dr, Chancellor Winchester
Hoby (late) Rev. Sir Philip, Dean Ardfert

Hodge,

Hodge (late) Rev. Dr
Hoghton, Sir Henry, Bart
Home, Right Honourable and Rev. Earl
Honywood (late) Frafer, Efq;
Howard, John, Efq;
Hume, Right Rev. Lord Bifhop Salifbury
Hunt, Rev. Dr, Regius Profeffor Hebrew, Oxford
Hunt, Henry, Efq; Tipperary
Hunter, Dr William
Hutchinfon, Francis, Efq; Dublin

Jane, Rev. Mr Jofeph
Jenkinfon, Charles, Efq;
Jennings (late) Rev. Dr
Jefus College, Oxford
Innys, John, Efq;
Johnfon, Right Rev. Lord Bifhop Worcefter
Jones, Mrs Mary
Jubb, Rev. Dr

Kaye, Rev. Mr, Sub-Almoner
Keene, Right Rev. Lord Bifhop Chefter
Kings College
Kippis, Rev. Dr
Kynafton, Thomas, Efq;

Lambe

Lambe (late) James, Efq;

Laugher (late) Rev. Mr

Lawfon, Rev. Mr

Lee, Matthew, Efq;

Legge (late) Right Honourable Henry Bilfon

Legh, Rev. Dr, Halifax

Ligonier, Right Honourable Earl

Litchfield, Right Honourable Earl

Llewelin, Thomas, Efq;

Long, Rev. Dr, Mafter Pembroke Hall

Loveday, John, Efq;

Loveday, John, Efq; Jun.

Lowth, Right Rev. Lord Bifhop Oxford

Lowther, Robert, Efq;

Lucas, Thomas, Efq;

Lyndon, William, Efq; Dublin

Lyttelton (late) Right Rev. Lord Bifhop Carlifle

Macclesfield (late) Right Honourable Earl

Madan, Rev. Mr Martin

Mallet, Rev. Mr, Preb. Gloucefter

Markham, Rev. Dr, Dean Chrift-Church

Markham, Rev. Dr, Whitechapel

Marlborough, His Grace, Duke

Martyn, Rev. Mr, Profeffor Botany, Cambridge

Mawfon, Right Rev. Lord Bifhop Ely

Maxwell,

Maxwell, Hon. & Right Rev. Lord Bifhop Meath
Meech (late) Thomas, Efq;
Melvill, Honourable General, Governor Granada
Merton College
Miles (late) Rev. Dr
Milles, Rev. Dr, Dean Exeter
Moore, Rev. Mr
Morton (late) Right Honourable Earl
Mofs, Right Rev. Lord Bifhop St David's
Mufgrave, Jofeph, Efq;

Nafh, Rev. Mr
Newcome (late) Right Rev. Lord Bifhop St Afaph
Newcome, Right Rev. Lord Bifhop Dromore
Newcome (late) Rev. Dr, Dean Rochefter
Newton, Right Rev. Lord Bifhop Briftol
Nicols, Rev. Dr
Norwich, Dean and Chapter

Ogle, Rev. Dr, Dean Winchefter
Oliver (late) Dr William
Onflow (late) Right Honourable Arthur
Ofbaldifton (late) Rt Rev. Lord Bifhop London

Paice, Jofeph, Efq;
Palke, Robert, Efq;

Parker,

Parker, Sir Thomas, Lord Chief Baron
Parker, Rev. Dr William
Parry, Rev. Mr
Pearce, Right Rev. Lord Bishop Rochester
Peck, Randyll, Esq;
Peploe, Rev. Dr, Warden Manchester
Peter House
Peters, Rev. Mr Charles
Pilkington (late) Rev. Mr
Plumptre, Rev. Archdeacon, D. D.
Pococke (late) Right Rev. Lord Bishop Ossory
Portall, Rev. Mr
Portland, His Grace, Duke
Potter, Rev. Dr, Dean Canterbury
Price (late) Robert, Esq;
Price, Rev. Mr Richard
Priest, Rev. Mr
Prime, Sir Samuel, Kt
Pringle, Sir John, Bart
Prior, Rev. Mr
Pyle, Rev. Dr, Preb. Winchester

Queen's College, Cambridge

Radnor, Right Honourable Earl
Randolph, Rev. Archdeacon, D. D.

Ratcliffe,

Ratcliffe, Rev. Dr, Mafter Pembroke College
Reynell, Rev. Mr
Rickards, Mr Samuel
Robinfon, His Grace, Lord Primate Ireland
Rockingham, Moft Noble Marquis
Rofe, Mr, Chifwick
Ryder, His Grace, Lord Arch-Bifhop Tuam

St Aubyn, Sir John, Bart
Salter, Rev. Dr, Mafter Charter Houfe
Salvadore, Jofeph, Efq;
Sanford, Rev. Mr Jofeph
Savage, Rev. Dr
Saunders, Rev. Dr Erafmus
Scrope, Rev. Dr
Secker (late) His Grace, Lord A-Bp Canterbury
Shaftefbury, Right Honourable Earl
Sherlock (late) Right Rev. Lord Bifhop London
Smalbroke, Rev. Mr Samuel
Smith, Rev. Mr
Spry, Dr Edward
Squire (late) Right Rev. Lord Bifhop St David's
Stallard, Mr, Clapham
Stanley, Honourable and Rev. Dr
Stennet, Rev. Dr
Stonehoufe, Rev. Dr, Briftol

Suffield,

Suffield, Thomas, Efq;

Suffolk and Berkfhire, Right Honourable Earl

Swinney, Rev. Dr

Swinton, Archibald, Efq;

*T*albot, Right Honourable Earl

Talbot, Hon. and Rev. Dr George

Talbot, Rev. Mr William, Clare - Hall

Talbot, Rev. Mr William, Reading

Tayler, Rev. Mr

Taylor (late) Rev. Dr, Chancellor Lincoln

Taylor (late) Charles, Efq;

Taylor, Rev. Mr George

Terrick, Right Rev. Lord Bifhop London

Territ, Rev. Mr

Thomas, Right Rev. Lord Bifhop Winchefter

Thomas (late) Right Rev. Lord Bifhop Salifbury

Thomas, Rev. Dr, Dean Weftminfter

Thompfon, Rev. Mr

Thornton, John, Efq;

Thorold, Sir John, Bart

Toller, Rev. Mr

Tomkins, Benjamin, Efq;

Tomkins, Jofeph, Efq;

Tomkins, William, Efq;

Townfhend, Honourable Thomas, Efq;

Trail,

Trail, Right Rev. Lord Bifhop Down and Connor

Trevor, Hon. & Right Rev. Lord Bifhop Durham

Turner (late) Sir Edward, Bart

Turner, Sir Gregory, Bart

Turner, Rev. Mr

Twynihoe, Rev. Mr

Tyrawly, Right Honourable Lord

Vaughan, Samuel, Efq;

Walker, Rev. Dr

Warner, Richard, Efq;

Warren (late) Rev. Mr

Weftfield, Mr Robert

Webb, Philip Carteret, Efq;

Webber, Rev. Dr, Dean Hereford

Wegg, George, Efq;

Wegg, Samuel, Efq;

Wells, Dean and Chapter

Weftminfter, Dean and Chapter

Wefton, Right Honourable Edward

Wefton, Rev. Mr, Preb. Durham

Wheeler, Rev. Mr, Profeffor Poetry, Oxford

Whitchurch, James, Efq;

Whitchurch, Rev. Mr Samuel

Wilberfofs, John, Efq;

Wills,

Wills, Right Rev. Lord Bifhop Bath and Wells
Winchefter, Dean and Chapter
Windfor, Dean and Chapter
Wollafton, Rev. Mr George
Wombwell, George, Efq;
Wood, Robert, Efq;
Worcefter, Dean and Chapter
Wray, Daniel, Efq;
Wrey, Sir Bouchier, Bart

Yarborough, Rev. Dr, Principal Brafe-Nofe Coll.
Yarborough, Rev. Dr, Tewing
Yonge, Right Rev. Lord Bifhop Norwich
Yorke, Honourable Charles, Efq;
Young, Right Rev. Lord Bifhop Leighlin & Ferns
Young (late) Rev. Dr Edward

✳ ✳ ✳ ✳ ✳ ✳ ✳ ✳ ✳ ✳ ✳ ✳

Anonymous . C.

Anonymous . F.

Anonymous . P.

Anonymous . P.

Anonymous . S.

Anonymous . T.

Anonymous . W.

* * * * * * * * * * * * *

P A T R O N E S S

Mrs ELIZABETH GRIFFEN

By A Legacy

200 £.

* * * * * * * * * * * * * *
* * * * * * * * * * * * * *

THE Delegates of the Prefs, in the Univerfity of Oxford, and alfo the Univerfity of Cambridge, having ordered, that the Continuance of their Subfcription to Dr Kennicott's Work fhould depend on a Certificate from me, as to a proper Progrefs annually made therein; and the Teftimony, which I have with great pleafure becaufe with great juftice granted, in the Nine former Years, having given me a public Connection with this Work: I apprehend, that my Name cannot at this time be at all improper.

My former Atteftations, together with the occafion of them, are now at an end. And there can be no neceffity for me to confirm what Dr Kennicott himfelf hath fet forth, in the Tenth and laft Account, as to his Undertaking being now completed. All that I intend therefore, after expreffing my entire conviction of the Truth and Exactnefs, with which the laft Account hath been ftated, is publickly to congratulate, as I do moft heartily, all the Patrons of this Work, together with the Conductor of it, on its being brought to a Conclufion. And I cannot but add my fincere Wifhes, that the very great Importance of it, of which I am myfelf fully convinced, may be proved as foon as poffible to the World, by the publication of a Work, which does fo much Honour to our Country in general, and to this Univerfity in particular.

THO. HUNT,

Regius Profeffor of Hebrew.

INDEX.

INDEX. 195

Aberdeen University; page 30.

Acad. Inscrip. & Belles Lettres; pag. 124.

Africa; pag. 76, 129, 153, 161.

Albani, Cardinal; pag. 28, 49, 60, 87, 88.

America; pag. 76, 129, 161.

Annual Account of the Collation; pag. 5, 6 &c.

Antient Versions; pag. 18, 22, 25, 142, 146.

A Porta, Prof. pag. 29, 51, 63, 73, 98, 127, 161.

Asia; pag. 76, 153, 162.

Asseline, Abbé, Sorbonne; pag. 118, 128, 159.

Assemani, Monsgr, Rome; pag. 49, 50.

Assistants; pag. 26, 45, 80, 163, 164.

Baden-Durlac, Margrave; pag. 97, 102, 112.

Bahrdt, Professor, Erfurt; pag. 160.

Ballarini, Librarian, Rome; pag. 60, 74.

Bartoli, Signr, Flor. pag. 29, 50, 63, 87, 115.

Barton, Dr; pag. 125.

Bayer, Don F. Toledo; pag. 30, 61.

Beauchamp, Lord Viscount; pag. 26.

Bejot, Libr. R. Paris; pag. 120.

Bengelius; pag. 68, 165.

Bernstorff, Count; pag. 71, 83, 96, 115, 127, 153.

Berretta, Padr. Flor. pag. 29, 50, 63, 87, 115.

Bertier, Pere, Orat. Paris; pag. 121.

Bible, interleaved, 30 vol. pag. 81.

Bibles, Hebrew, printed; pag. 25, 82, 85, 95,
99—106, 111, 113. 130, 140, 143, 147.

Bibles, Hebrew, corrupted; pag. 7, 25, 99.

Botta, Marshal; pag. 28.

A a   Branca,

Jablonſki's

                                                    Richardfon,

Van